TRAPPED

TRAPPED

NEGLECTED, ABUSED, BETRAYED

DELLA WRIGHT
WITH LINDA WATSON-BROWN

jb

First published in the UK by John Blake Publishing
An imprint of Bonnier Books UK
4th Floor, Victoria House,
Bloomsbury Square,
London, WC1B 4DA

Owned by Bonnier Books
Sveavägen 56, Stockholm, Sweden

www.facebook.com/johnblakebooks 𝗳
twitter.com/jblakebooks 𝕏

Paperback ISBN: 978-1-789-465-12-9
Ebook ISBN: 978-1-789-465-13-6
Audiobook ISBN: 978-1-789-465-14-3

A CIP catalogue of this book is available from the British Library.

Designed by Envy Design Ltd
Printed and bound by Clays Ltd, Elcograf S.p.A.

1 3 5 7 9 10 8 6 4 2

Copyright © Della Wright and Linda Watson-Brown, 2022

Della Wright and Linda Watson-Brown have asserted their moral right to be
identified as the authors of this Work in accordance with the Copyright,
Designs and Patents Act 1988.

John Blake Publishing is an imprint of Bonnier Books UK
www.bonnierbooks.co.uk

For little Della – you made it x

CONTENTS

PROLOGUE

October 1975

Something terrible was happening at the front door, *to* the front door. A banging the likes of which I'd never heard before. The sound was made worse by the rain beating on the window of my bedroom, making everything seem scary, making everything seem that much more terrifying.

Two-year-old me cowered further into the recesses of my bed, crying and shaking. My arms were wrapped around my knees and I was trying not to imagine what could possibly come next, but the racket was relentless. I squeezed my eyes tightly shut, but although that closed out a lot, it didn't stop the pounding in my ears.

My baby brother was wailing in his cot next to me, a noise that wouldn't stop, a noise that had been going on for what felt like hours. He was always crying and there never seemed to be anyone there to make it better.

I could hear shouting and the sense that someone was hitting the door time after time. *THUD. THUD. THUD. THUD. THUD.* A crash made it sound as if it had finally given way and I heard footsteps running into our flat.

People came into my room and I sensed someone standing over me. Using every ounce of bravery I had, I opened my eyes and looked at the group of uniformed officers who were staring at the sight of me – skinny, neglected, dirty, alone. Little more than a baby, little more than a scrap of life.

'Della?' the policewoman closest to me asked. 'Della? Are you OK, love? Where's your mummy? Can you tell us where your mummy is, Della?'

No. No, I couldn't. I had no idea where my mummy was – only that when she was there, things were even worse.

STORIES

That's my first memory. Not a favourite dolly, not someone singing me a lullaby, but the police using a battering ram to get into the high-rise flat where Mum had left us alone. It can't have been the first time, but I think it was the final straw for a neighbour who contacted the police. They must have seen Mum do it on previous occasions – heard two tiny children cry all night and decided that this time something had to be done.

I'm sure there would have been other moments that weren't out of a perfect parent guidebook, but that one is stuck in my memory bank. Even if I close my eyes now, I can see the flat where I was left alone in my cot, my baby brother at the side of me, both left in stinking filled nappies, with empty stomachs, every shred of us neglected. The flat was a testament to that neglect. The carpets were black sticky-backed tiles which had been haphazardly attached to parts of the floor, there was a rancid cat litter tray which was never emptied, dirt everywhere, cans and tins left on kitchen surfaces and not a single toy in the whole place. I wouldn't have been playing when the police came in, nor would I be holding a beloved teddy, because I had nothing apart from my imagination.

From the first part of my life that I can recall, I would make up games in my head and disappear to other worlds. My favourite imaginary adventure was to pretend I was in a spaceship with dials on the wall that I could press. These dials would make the world in my head change colour or shape, they would make it sunny or give me a sky full of stars. I could choose whether to be alone or surrounded by strange little alien creatures, whether to go to the moon or visit another planet. Wherever I went, and whoever went with me, would be something I held onto when real life crept in. The dials on the wall gave me everything as long as I could imagine it. In reality, there were no dials, there wasn't anything I could touch at all. It was all in my head because I was never given anything. I know that lots of families were – and are – poor, but children are creative; they'll play with empty boxes, making them into castles or caves. They'll draw on the backs of envelopes with a scrap of pencil worn down to the nub or make new worlds from hanging blankets on a clothes horse. Those are such little things and I didn't even have them.

I still wanted to play, though. What child doesn't? To this day, I've got burn marks on my thighs from when I would get all of the things out of the kitchen cupboard to make pretend cakes – caustic soda being one of them. It would drip down on me as I tried to make something, pretend it was icing sugar, left alone no matter the consequences. I was never really supervised because I had a mother who was completely disinterested. I don't know whether she was drunk or out when I made those 'cakes', or whether she was just completely unbothered about what I was up to, but the thought that a little girl would only have that to enjoy breaks my heart.

From when I was a year old, I was already known to Social Services. A 'Request for Advice/Assistance' form from October 1974, when I was less than 18 months old, simply states, *marital problems*. In more detail later on, the report says, *husband irresponsible – stays out nights. She (Mum) was thinking of getting a separation at one time. Debt in family – 3 weeks rent arrears, Husband comes in drunk sometimes.*

It seems so bland written down like that, but those

words hide more neglect and dysfunction than you might think. All of these records, all of these memories, have been a jigsaw I've had to piece together. Not everyone gets their records, despite there being legislation in place to allow access. Many are lost in fires as they are paper copies from decades ago, some disappear when offices are relocated. On occasion, they can be so heavily redacted that nothing makes sense. I've trawled through all of mine, each revelation making a little more sense, but also shocking me. There is so much minimising, from all sides, and yet also a great deal of awareness of what was going on – although it was virtually all ignored. As I've put together the information in those files with the stories held in my own mind and body, a terrible picture has emerged.

In April 1975, six months before the police stormed into the flat, my dad was convicted of armed robbery and received a four-year sentence. In August, Mum had an abortion as the baby clearly wasn't his given that he was in jail, all of it part of a story that needs to be unpicked a little more. It wasn't long after that when reports started to be made about the fact that I was left alone in the flat quite often – I was only about two and a half at that point. On 20 October 1975, two neighbours made the report about it and once the police were in and had checked my brother and I were safe, one of those neighbours took me to her flat.

Mum didn't return until nearly midnight, drunk and unsteady. With Dad still in prison for four years on the robbery charge, I suspect she was out with other men rather than friends, especially given what I now know of her having an abortion. *The flat was untidy. There were traces of vomit on the living room floor. The kitchen was foul-smelling, with cat remains on the floor.*

* * *

How had we got to that point? My mum, Carol, was born into a chaotic, broken family – to some extent, just like the one she would create. Her father had 13 children, to lots of different women, but his first batch was all to his first wife. When he met the woman who I would think of as Nan until I discovered the truth in my teenage years, he upped sticks and took a few of his children with him. One of those was Mum. Grandad had been a bus driver and he'd met my step-nan on one of his routes when she was a 'clippie' (as conductresses were called in those days). He seemed to have no hesitation in leaving his wife or kids and I don't really know why he bothered to take some of them with him to his new life. In fact, I don't really know the truth in a lot of the stories Mum has told me over the years.

An expert in gaslighting before anyone even had a

word for it, she revelled in telling me one thing on a Monday and twisting it round by the Tuesday. It was hard to know which way was which, so when she said she'd been taken into care as a baby, I believed her. She also claimed that her stepmother didn't want her as she was too young and needed a lot of attention, which meant she was given up almost as soon as she got there. I was told lots of stories of how she spent years in care, always hoping her dad would come back for her, which he did from time to time, before her evil stepmother sent her away again. Eventually, they moved Mum to a different area so that she wouldn't keep absconding from the care home to try and be with them. Was it true? I have no idea – but the records I have suggest not.

Carol Wright (née Walker) came into the care of Social Services when she was 11 years old. Her father and cohabitee cared for her until this time. When Carol was 11, her father remarried, but Carol refused to leave his cohabitee, who she knew as her mother. Apparently, her relationship with her father had always been poor. However, since she had a history of absconding from home, she was not allowed to remain in the care of this woman and consequently was admitted to a children's home.

That is a very different story to the one I was told. Mum never suggested to me that she was close to Nan, that she saw her as a mother and didn't want to leave her once her Dad found another woman and went on his merry way again.

My paternal grandfather had died when my own dad, Arthur, was young. His mum ended up bringing up six kids on her own. Being in trouble was always in Dad's nature, maybe through having no father as a role model, and it increased until he started getting on the wrong side of the law. He left school when he was only 13 and started work as a butcher, which was the beginning of him taking on any job that presented itself really, just to earn a bit of money. He was basically a cheeky bugger all his life. Mum worked in Woolworths when they met and he used to go up to her once he'd finished work and ask for a bag of sweets and a flash of her drawers! She was only 17 at this point and he was a couple of years older. He did a bit of everything to earn some cash but at the time they met he was working in a sex shop, which made Mum mortally embarrassed any evening she went to meet him there after his shift.

Mum was very pretty, blonde and slim, whereas Dad, with his black, thick wiry hair and beard was a bit of a hippy, with flared trousers and big collars, a real seventies stereotype. Mum was of that time too in her own way and I remember her wearing miniskirts with a real two-tone Mod sort of vibe. They went to a lot of dances together but she later told me that wasn't as straightforward as you might think. She was very upfront about wanting a black boyfriend as she wasn't interested in white men at all – this statement alongside Dad's racism went as well as you can imagine and he would call her terrible names for all of their time together, frequently based on the fact that she always said she hated him because he wasn't black (alongside plenty of other reasons). She really was never that bothered about him, but Dad always said she was the love of his life.

Mum got pregnant with me very quickly, so that she could get out of the care system I've been told, but again, there is a discrepancy between the other stories I was fed and the records. She said to me that she turned down Dad's proposal until just a couple of weeks before I was born and never wanted to marry him; he wore her down and she gave in because he was an escape from the care system. Was that true, or was the official line the one that told the tale of my beginnings?

[she] remained in care until her marriage. Carol met Arthur Wright when she was 17 years old. The Department refused to give Carol permission to marry him, so she became pregnant to force their hand. Apparently, Carol saw marriage as a solution to all her problems, but her relationship with her husband started to deteriorate after Della's birth. Mr Wright wanted a boy and was quick to express his

displeasure about Della. He showed little interest in his daughter and started going out regularly, indulging in heavy drinking. Mr Wright gave his wife little or no support, ran up debts, and, at times, showed violence towards her.

Mum was 18 when she gave birth to me in May 1973 and it was obvious from the start that she and Dad were just too young to be married or parents. Despite him claiming he loved her so much, he would disappear for days at a time, coming back with love bites which he flaunted and stories of what he had been doing with other women. Dad was in prison at the time of the police raid on the 15th-floor flat – but when he was there, he was much more affectionate than Mum. I know that he was the one who organised one of the few happy family memories I have. He had family up North and wc went on a beach trip one summer, building sandcastles, holding hands jumping over cracks in the pavements, just being a normal Mum, Dad and two kids. I don't have many memories like that, which makes the few I do have all the more precious.

The warmest person I had in my life was Mum's step-nanny (Nan's Mum). She was such a lovely lady, she'd take people in off the streets if they were struggling, and she always had hugs for me. I called her Great Nan. She was probably the kindest, warmest person in my world, making up at times for the volatile home life I had. Again, I don't know how many of the stories were true but Mum said that Dad used to wake me up in the middle of the night to watch him beat her, but I can't remember any of that. If it was true, then no wonder I clung to any sense of normality when I saw Great Nan. My parents had a lot of debts and Mum was always claiming that she was going to separate and divorce Dad, painting a picture of him as a horrible man, whereas he would remind her of all the good things he had done. Who knows what to believe? Records say about Mum:

From the age of ten years, Carol has been involved with the Social Services Department, and has been in many children's homes. She is emotionally immature and is a great manipulator. She alters the truth of situations so that it suits her needs and so that she is the one who is often deserving of sympathy. She doesn't see herself as being wrong in any situation nor will she take the responsibility for her own actions.

That certainly fits with the mum I knew, the one who left me in the flat while she went out drinking and spending time with men who weren't my father. I assume that's what she must have been doing the night she left me and my brother in the flat alone, as she'd done before, and I assume that the neighbour who looked after me that night had just had enough of it all.

I spent the night with her, then was officially

admitted into the care of a woman called Mrs Abdul the next morning. I don't really remember any of that. Apparently, when Mum got back to the flat and found the police there, her children gone and the authorities alerted, she went ballistic. She tried every excuse in the book, but it was clear that she had gone over a line. Her response was to do something which would become very typical of her in years to come – she brought all of the attention back to her and how she was being treated, how everything was unfair and she just couldn't go on if people didn't do what she wanted.

The next day, she took a Valium overdose. The files say that Mum was confused about what had happened but finally admitted to things 'getting on top of her'. She also admitted that she had borrowed some money from a friend the night before and left for the pub at 7pm, leaving me in bed as she closed the door behind her. As a mother myself, it beggars belief that she could have thought this was fine. She must have known she would be out for hours and that a two-year-old in bed at that time of night in an empty house would be in potential danger.

It's hard not to let my imagination run to what I must have been thinking or feeling. Two and a half years old is still so tiny. It's the age when you are barely out of being a baby, when you still need cuddles if you cry. The world is a scary place and being alone feels terrifying. It mustn't have mattered to her. My brother was even younger, but she left us both and went off drinking. I don't know whether she would have just assumed we would have been alright or whether her reasoning was even worse; perhaps she thought that if something did happen to us, it wouldn't be that much of a big deal anyway.

The report after that event says that Mum looked:

... tired and depressed. She told me that she isn't sleeping well and often dreams of falling off the veranda. She often contemplates going into a chemist and buying some tablets. Her husband was violent towards her and she told me one day he had put Della in a gas oven and threw her favourite cat over the balcony. Her fear is of being lonely.

And it was that fear which would ruin my life more than she had managed to do so far. Mum always wanted someone. She always wanted a man. The man of her dreams would worship her, tell her she was beautiful and that every other man wanted her. But most of all, I think, that he would take her away from what she hated most of all and that was being a mother.

2

PILLAR TO POST

Any memories I do have of my very early life come in snippets. When I add them to the Social Services records I have, a picture does build. It's an unhappy one, littered with neglect and misery. Some parts don't even seem to make sense to the adults involved.

In August 1976, the files show that the social worker assigned to our family received a call from the police, who said that Mum had taken another overdose. This was a really common occurrence – from what I can tell, it was usually a combination of any medication she could lay her hands on, painkillers and alcohol. I had been left alone, with my little brother, as usual. The social worker notes that she had seen Mum the week before and everything seemed fine; she impresses on the police that they have to keep her up to date with everything (I assume she means reports of us being left alone).

There are so many unanswered questions here. Who discovered that Mum had taken an overdose? Who called the police? Why, when the police say she was taken to hospital, can the social worker find no record of Mum when she calls? Where were we taken? When did we go back and why was that allowed? Overdoses never seemed to work for Mum, no matter how many she tried, and I do have to wonder whether it was just for attention. I have even wondered if she took them in the first place, or as many as she claimed, or whether the social workers and police were just manipulated into thinking they'd happened.

For a year, it had been more of the same – being left alone, overdoses, social workers doing nothing, neighbours reporting neglect. Then, in October 1976, the police had to break into the flat again and we were admitted on an eight-day Place of Safety Order. My brother and I were sent to The Lyndens Children's Home and Mum was admitted to hospital. After a week, she was transferred to a psychiatric hospital and we were sent to a foster home, living with a woman called Mrs Miller.

Mrs Miller was horrible. She would leave my brother to scream in his bunk bed and just close the door when he was bothering her. If we were both crying, she would switch the lights off so that we were left crying in the dark. Despite how Mum was, how neglectful she was, I wanted her: she was all I knew and she was my mother. I just wanted home. It didn't seem as if we were being treated much better and I would rather it was her who was doing it than this horrible woman who had no idea what was meant when she was asked to 'care' for us.

'If you don't stop screaming, you'll never see your bloody mother again!' Mrs Miller would yell. She was vile. She had more guinea pigs than I could count (not that I could really count at all) and they absolutely stank. Those filthy creatures were in an open cage, not locked in, and would run about wherever they wanted, doing the toilet everywhere and scaring me half to death that they would bite me as they ran wild. The smell was much worse than our cat or its litter tray and it used to make me gag.

Mrs Miller was very pleased about the fact that she took in poor, neglected children like us. We'd go out for walks, with my brother in a pram, while she stopped to talk to everyone and tell them about us. They would all say what an angel she was; she'd smile, basking in their approval, then take us back to shout some more about how unappreciative we were and how we'd never see our mother at this rate. I think she was just in it to be seen as some sort of amazing person who took in poor kids, but I suspect the money came in useful too. She did keep us clean and fed, but it was definitely just a job to her.

One day, Mrs Miller got us up and dressed earlier than usual.

'You're going out today,' she said.

'Are we going for a walk?' I asked her. That was pretty much all she did so that she could get the kind words from other people.

'No – nothing to do with me,' she huffed. 'Your social worker's coming.'

'Why?' I wanted to know. I would have had no idea what a social worker was, but, like most children of that age, I tended to ask *why?* a million times a day.

'Always a hundred bloody questions with you, isn't it? Well, if you must know, you're going to see your mother. Maybe that will shut you up.'

I was so excited at the sound of the word 'mother'! It would definitely shut me up if I could get my mum back. 'Where's Mum? Where's Mum?' I wanted to know.

'She's in a mental institution – no surprises there,' I was informed. I had no idea what that was, she could have been speaking another language. 'Sit there,' she snapped. 'Social worker's coming.'

All I could feel was a bubbling excitement that I was going to see Mum. I had no idea what a 'mental institution' was and I can only piece this all together from the records I have now, but I would know better than to ask any more questions of Mrs Miller. I remember sitting on a chair at the front door, jiggling my leg up and down with nerves. I know that I would have thought, if I was getting my mummy again, surely I wouldn't have to come back here? Surely once she saw me, she'd keep me with her.

The doorbell rang and my foster mum – as I guess that's what Mrs Miller was – ran to the door, smoothing down her apron and patting her hair into place. 'Speak when you're spoken to,' she hissed at me, before welcoming the young woman in with a big smile.

'So lovely to see you!' she simpered. 'Della is thrilled that you are taking the time to visit her mother today. She's *very* grateful.'

'Right. Come on then,' were the only words spoken in reply. The social worker took my hand and only answered my questions about her name after a few tries. 'Grace. Get in the car, let's go see your mother.' Her lack of chattiness didn't bother me too much as I probably made up for both of us on the trip there.

'Have you seen my mum?' I asked. 'Do you go to visit her? Is she excited to see me? I'm excited to see her. Does she have a nice house, or are we going back to my old house? It smells there. Does it still smell there? Has Mum cleaned it, or is there somewhere new? I'd like a garden. Is there a garden? Is Mum in the garden?'

'She's in hospital,' Grace finally replied. 'I thought Mrs Miller told you that. I asked her to. I asked her to prepare you.'

Prepare me for what? I didn't need preparation for seeing Mum or for going home. It never occurred to me that we would be going somewhere else, to a strange place where Mum would not be the mother I wanted or needed – not that she ever had been. As the car slowed down, all I could see were high walls that seemed to go on forever. It definitely wasn't my house – looking back, I know that it was a Victorian building in its own grounds and had been an asylum for many years. Grace got me out of the car once we'd parked and took me through a long hallway into what seemed like a doctor's waiting room. It was huge. There were chairs placed along all of the walls and a scattering of people. I scanned the room until I found her and with happiness, ran over to the chair where she sat.

'Mummy!' I cried.

But she didn't stop talking to the woman sitting next to her. It was as if she couldn't even acknowledge that I was in her lap. From records, I discovered that she had been undergoing electroconvulsive therapy (ECT), where electric shocks would have been passed through her brain to start seizures in the hope that the treatment would also change her brain enough to reverse her depression, or whatever else they had decided was wrong.

Mum wasn't herself, I soon realised. She kept talking to the woman next to her about the treatment, about the electric shocks, and I had this notion that the doctors had been putting lightbulbs in her mouth. I've no idea where it came from but I was so worried she would get hurt by it, that she would swallow some of the glass. She was disorientated and unable to focus, I know that, and she wasn't interested in me at all. Even the social worker tried to initiate some sort of interaction.

'Look, Carol, here's Della,' she kept saying. 'She's doing well, she's safe and being looked after.' Mum turned her head to look at Grace as if she'd just realised that she was there, but there was no response. 'You'll have been worried about her, I bet? Nothing to worry about now – look, Carol, look, it's Della.' There was no point; she only got a glazed look and no engagement whatsoever. All Mum wanted to do was chat to the woman at the side of her and keep repeating that she'd had electric shocks put through her.

We returned to Mrs Miller and I felt like I'd never see my mum again. God knows how, or why, but whoever was in charge must have decided that everything was fine, because I was sent back to Mum just six days later. She must have seemed better to whoever discharged her, capable of being a mum again, but I don't remember the details. I was just happy to be with her again. Exactly a month later, in December 1976, a Supervision Order was made on me by Birmingham Juvenile Court and this was meant to last for three years. The only other change was that I was given nursery sessions at Nechells Day Care Centre to give Mum a break on some occasions. There are Records of Complaint from those days too. On one occasion, I was found to have burns on me but nothing was done. Mum said she didn't know how they happened until admitting it might have been because of the electric fire. She was told to get a fireguard but dismissed the suggestion, saying that the fire wouldn't be an issue soon as she couldn't pay the electricity bill. The next visit to check up on me didn't go ahead as she didn't answer the door and the next one was a waste of time as a neighbour was there with her two children so no questions could be asked because of confidentiality.

By January 1977, there had been another report and the senior social worker wrote that I was 'at risk'. After I had gone back to day care after Christmas, I had more burns and yet again, Mum had no explanation for them. When I started going to Barnardo's, I loved it. However, I was too little to know why I was attending sessions all of a sudden – that they were checking to see if I was neglected or hurt – all I knew was that it was a lovely place to be. There was one young woman called Carolyn who worked there and she seemed to have a particular soft spot for me. It would never happen now, but there were often times when she took me home with her once the nursery session was over. She lived with her parents and the whole family was so kind. It was the sort of world I'd never seen and I wished it was mine. Carolyn even kept me for sleepovers – unthinkable really! – and those were the happiest times I had at that point. She was so caring and lovely, the house was clean and warm, everything about it was just perfect. I'd come down in the morning to a plate of hot, buttered toast on the table that her mum had made. The Bee Gees would be playing in the background and the whole family laughed among each other. Until that point, I hadn't known that people could live like that.

The ongoing reports noted that I was often 'sniffly and seem to get little fresh air', but that I did 'well at nursery where people make a fuss' of me. Mum was openly telling them about her numerous boyfriends at this stage and it was often recorded: 'What I'd really like is a soldier,' is one of the comments in the files. She was constantly changing her mind as to whether she wanted Dad back or not, whether she wanted a divorce or not, and I do wonder if it was partly to keep the attention of the social workers. Was she winding them up or was she just feeling completely selfish and not bothered about the repercussions of looking like a terrible mother? Probably a bit of both.

There is talk in the records of Dad coming home once he was on parole, but Mum wasn't keen. Reports at this time mention that she had numerous boyfriends, that she thought she was pregnant at one point and that she wanted rid of the baby. It turned out that she was never pregnant but she did manage to create a lot of drama, which had the social worker telling her the dangers of trying to abort on her own. I can only imagine what would have happened in that meeting, with Mum insistent she was pregnant and just as insistent that she was going to do a home abortion. Knowing what she was like, I can just see her in my mind, loving being the centre of attention, probably well aware that she was spinning them all a tale rather than actually thinking she was pregnant in the first place. The records show that she had 'VD' (venereal disease as sexually transmitted infections (STIs) were called back then), so there was a chance that she was simply trying to deflect their knowledge of that and win the sympathy vote as a struggling mum faced with the possibility of another baby on the way, so desperate for a solution that she would consider sticking a knitting needle up inside or throwing herself down some stairs.

It is quite remarkable to see some of the comments made – and to know that there was nothing done.

Mum told the social worker that she feared she would be 'too violent' with me if I was naughty, that she often felt like hitting me 'very hard', but still no action was taken. By this time, I'd had bruises on my head and body, burns on my hands and feet, and there had been multiple reports of me and my brother being left alone. During this time and the years that followed, it seems there was a lot more attention paid to the fact that Mum was always behind on her gas bill than her child being neglected.

Later in 1977, Mum complained that neighbours were calling her a 'slut' and the social worker agreed that they had cause to do so if they were seeing multiple men visit while her husband was in prison! Mum was obviously useless with money as she was constantly threatened with eviction because of rent arrears and the social workers often had to bail her out with electricity and gas bills too. She was given clothes donations for me and my brother but, overall, there is a sense from the reports that she took no responsibility for anything really. Around this time, it was also suggested that Mum come into nursery two days a week to be with me in a controlled environment. She showed 'worry that the nursery staff will judge her if she is at the end of her tether' with me but was told that I would be diverted if that happened. She thinks she will be being 'watched' – it seems to me like that would have been a very good idea indeed. At least once a month, neighbours report that I have been left alone in the flat. On one occasion in October 1975, the police broke in, admitting me to care and placing me on an eight-day Place of Safety Order. By the time the Order expired, Mum was back in hospital with depression and I was back in care.

An update on the November 1975 Supervision Order was made in October 1976. I was clearly often left unattended and admitted to The Lyndens Children's Home for just one day before being transferred back to Mrs Miller in Tamworth, Staffordshire. My records show that my Place of Safety Order expired eight days later, but Mum was still in hospital after her latest overdose, which meant that the horrible – but safe – Mrs Miller would have to look after me for a bit longer. I was discharged after five weeks with her, although a Supervision Order was still in place.

It's exhausting reading the back and forth of care, home, care, home, care, home – and it didn't end there. Mum was readmitted to hospital in January 1977 and I was with Mrs Miller for 11 days again. I had actually been found unattended by social workers a lot, even when I was at home, with a multitude of referrals recorded between 1975 and 1976, and I must have felt relief at being back with the foster carer after all that.

It is very clear to me that I should have been removed permanently at that point. Even with the three-year

Supervision Order that had been granted, I was still left alone on so many occasions, neglected and put at constant risk. My only safety was when I was given to other women who fostered me, my only escape when I was taken away from my own mother. It is obvious from the records that I was checked regularly when I was at home and that, at this point of my life, the Social Services Department and Barnardo's worked closely together to ensure my safeguarding, but to me, they didn't do enough for me or my brother.

A report about Mum at the time said: 'Carol is quite an attractive girl, who has slimmed considerably over the last few months. She is inclined to be negative and easily depressed but at times of crisis she tends to ask for approval of the way she's dealt with it, rather than actually asking what to do, e.g. the VD clinic.' Another said: 'The Wright family are very well known to this Department. Social work intervention had not proved effective in the past. Mrs Wright was described to me by the Team Leader as an immature, manipulative liar who would never accept responsibility for her own actions.'

Very well known to this Department.

An immature, manipulative liar.

Never accept responsibility.

It was all there in black and white, but none of it seemed to be ringing the right alarm bells.

3

SPACESHIPS AND DAYDREAMS

When I was about four, there were times when Mum took me to see Dad in jail and it was very similar to when I had been to visit her in the psychiatric institutions. We would walk into a big room, with tables as well as chairs, and Dad would be sat waiting. He always had on one of those stereotypical striped tops but what I remember most was that I used to get a twin pack of custard creams from the lady who had a trolley of drinks and snacks in the corner. I hated them then and I hate them now! Dad was always happy to see me and engaged much more than Mum ever did with me.

'I've missed you!' he would tell me. 'Now, are you being a good girl for your mum?'

'No, she bloody well is not,' Mum would reply. 'Never bloody leaves me alone, always hanging onto me whenever she's there. Can't get a minute to myself.'

She got plenty of minutes to herself – hours of them

– but it was never enough. She could never be out of the house enough, never away from me enough.

'Ah now, I'm sure that's not true – I'd love to be back home, I'd love to be there with her,' Dad answered. Was it just that he romanticised it all because he was in prison? Maybe. Probably. However, he'd always been the affectionate one, not that there was much competition. They just used to argue during those visits. It was such a noisy room, like a school dinner hall, and no one paid any notice to their shouting anyway. They certainly seemed to have no love for each other and with Dad in prison, Mum was free to meet other men.

She began a relationship with one particular bloke, Tony, very quickly and moved us in with him. She was a bit nicer round him, here was someone she could act out a certain role in front of and be a better mum. He was actually perfectly nice to me but his daughter – who must have been about seven or eight years old – was in a care home as she'd been abused. I don't know who had abused her but it seems unbelievable that Mum wouldn't think twice about putting her small child into such an environment. As had been the case with me being dragged to the psychiatric hospital where Mum was, and the prison where Dad was, I got taken to the care home where this little girl, Louisa, was living. It was another old Victorian, redbrick building and in the open space where everyone chatted, there were at least toys. I played with them as much as I could while we visited, desperately trying to make memories which would feed my imagination for the times when rooms were empty and days were long.

Mum became pregnant at this time. It wasn't something I was aware of but the files show she had an abortion while Dad was in jail. We stayed with Tony until Dad got out of prison. I have a vague memory of Dad coming looking for her and we all went back to the flat, which she'd kept on while she was with Tony, who disappeared from that point.

Everything was as it had been before between them. All I had was the bit of affection I got from Dad, which was at total odds with what Mum told the social workers. She was always saying to them, in front of me, that he had been disappointed I was a girl, that he resented it, yet I never got that feeling from him. She'd tell everyone actually, being especially keen to rub my nose in it.

To put it bluntly, Mum was a complete headfuck. She'd tell me one thing but it wouldn't fit with all the other things she'd said. Later on in life was when she'd tell me that Dad would get me up in the middle of the night to watch him beat her. I don't have any memories of that at all. She told me that her brother and his friend had looked after me one day and when she got back, I had the imprint of a Doc Marten boot on my back. Even if these things were true, why would she tell me, what could she hope to gain from it? It was almost as if she was laying down the foundations for me to be seen as someone whose memory couldn't be trusted, who said things that were untrue, and that chills me.

From the start of 1977, I was in and out of care after further Place of Safety Orders, released, discharged, readmitted, released, discharged … the same cycle was on repeat. I was just being passed from one environment to another, from Mum to care, over and over again. I don't know what they thought was going to change, or why they thought anything would alter dramatically without any proactive input. At the end of the year, I was back in care when Dad came out of prison, although he and Mum had officially separated by then.

The situation – my situation – was reviewed every six months and the picture painted of me then seemed acceptable on the surface. In fact, I seem like a perfect child. I was only four and a half years old. Reading between the lines would have shown a different story to the positive points they made:

General progress – sensitive, intelligent girl, very independent who can dress and undress apart from shoelaces. Needs no encouragement. Does not have a daytime sleep. Sits down to table without fuss. Is a steady eater, sometimes wants more, and has very good table manners. She relates well to staff, warm and affectionate, with no preferences. Responds to affection. Pleased to see Mum. Greets her and visitors but not upset when they leave. Della relates well to individual children, especially little ones whom she helps dress etc. Is motherly and protective.

I come across as a very well-balanced little girl. With regards to how I played when I was at day care, the picture drawn was very similar:

Shows evidence of initiative and imaginative play in the Wendy House and acts out the mother role. Enjoys creative play, especially painting. Well co-ordinated but quite nervous when climbing. She is not a clumsy child. Her fine muscle skills and concentration span quite good for her age and she gets absorbed in tasks, not easily distracted and does not like to be disturbed. Della's comprehension is good. Expressive language.

Dancing and music were my favourite things and I could easily lose myself in a little world of spinning around and singing. It was only a tiny bit of joy in my life, but it mattered so much.

The report did bring up the 'problem of bruising'.

Given that they already knew from Mum that she could be too violent and she sometimes hit me very hard, it is again unbelievable that the authorities simply accepted that I bruised 'easily'. I was on the 'At Risk' register at the day care centre and examined each morning for bruises, a fact which 'upset' Mum. This was discussed but it was 'resolved that it is in the interests of Della, her mother and DCC staff that this should remain'. Dad may have been out of prison by now but because he and Mum were separated, I still had no real home life. I'd never had a stable male figure in my life and this was noted in my files. It was also written that I 'presented a lot of behaviour problems at home', but on the word of my mother, that would be very subjective. In fact, anything which stopped her from living the life of a single woman would be seen as a problem.

Mum was given a Plan of Action which stated that she needed to take me to the Health Centre when I had serious bruises – if she didn't, then the nursery staff would, as long as she signed a letter allowing that. They emphasised that a relationship needed to develop between us and that preparation had to be made for starting school that Easter (in those days, there were two annual intakes).

Looking at my files (and by God, have I spent hours, days, weeks poring over them), some things hit me more than others. In 1978 there is a letter between the senior social worker at Barnardo's and the team leader of Social Services at Birmingham. It is all very friendly, they're on first-name terms, but there is one exchange that sticks out to me. While Mum is being castigated for day care arrears of £38.80, there is an unusual mention of my father – who has clearly made quite the impression on the Barnardo's lady (a woman who was under the impression that I was called 'Dellar' for some reason):

I should add that [Della's] father made a very valuable contribution at the Christmas Fayre and obviously has leadership potential! I believe the couple were re-united prior to Christmas and trust the situation is not too stormy at the present time.

Well, wouldn't it have been lovely if he had made a valuable 'contribution' to my day care fees, this man with leadership potential? My parents decided to get back together round about then, but like my revolving doors of care and discharge, their relationship was one of chaos and well-known mistakes being repeated.

I don't remember anyone telling me that it was going to happen, that I was going back to Mum. I do know that when any time I returned, she was just the same as ever, spending a lot of time in bed, doing nothing, or going out to get away from me. There was never any kindness or affection; I felt as if I was an inconvenience to her and yet I wanted her so badly. She was my mother and I needed her. I was so young that I felt she would change one day, she would become the type of Mummy that I knew existed in stories, that existed for other little girls, and all I had to do was be the right sort of child.

I did feel safe in Barnardo's and I loved Carolyn hugely, which made the gulf between how she was with me and Mum's treatment even more obvious. I was checked at playgroup every day and I know that they were looking out for any signs that Mum was incapable of keeping me. I do genuinely feel that although there were an awful lot of bruises, bumps and burns, she wasn't deliberately abusing me. It was neglect, pure and simple. All of the things they could see were just the consequences of a woman who couldn't care less about her child. I fell, I banged into things, I was alone so much – I was even still making my cakes out of what was under the sink and none of that even registered with her.

I was playing in my imagination as much as I could, making spaceships on the walls, dreaming of other lives, and I had no toys that I could remember at all. I hosted a lot of imaginary tea parties where I would pretend to be pouring out drinks into dainty cups and saucers for all my dolly and teddy friends, but there was nothing apart from what was in my head. There wasn't a single thing to play with in that house, it was just how life was. I was too little to have a sense of loneliness as such, although when Carolyn started taking me to her house, it became very painful. I didn't want to leave such a beautiful, clean, loving place – I could have lived there forever.

It was the only representation of normality I'd ever had in my life. Dad was often away and Mum kept telling me he didn't want me. She was completely neglectful and disinterested. My childhood up to that point was simply something to get through – I had no idea how much worse it could become.

4

REMEMBER MY NAME

Mum and Dad decided they would have a fresh start in 1978 too, so we moved house – but that only seemed to increase the friction between them. The new place in Aston, inner Birmingham, was only a couple of miles away from the high-rise flats and was a three-storey townhouse. Go in through the front door and there was a toilet on the left and a kitchen ahead, with a living room upstairs on the left and a bedroom on the right. Up another flight of stairs were two bedrooms and a bathroom. It was a very different space to what we were used to. When Mum and Dad were offered it by Birmingham City Council, the place was in a right state, but there was very little choice given – basically, they were told to take it or leave it. It's a pretty bad area now, but as a child, it was a great place to live, multi-cultural with Jamaican and Asian families as our neighbours and – the best thing – a garden.

This was meant to be Mum and Dad's brand-new beginning. Dad had got out of prison and she'd got out of her affair: it was all going to be perfect. It lasted very little time before it all went wrong. Dad was a bugger and always had other women on the go, but not long after we moved to Aston, he met someone who seemed to mean more to him than just a bit on the side. There were so many cracks in his relationship with Mum and I don't think it ever occurred to either of them that not sleeping with other people might help.

The Supervision Order for me had also expired and the new Social Services Area Office wasn't made sufficiently aware of the safeguarding issues (or perhaps they didn't give this enough attention). At this point there was clearly neglect but also injuries sustained which show in their reports as well as my medical records. Despite that, the case was closed. The records also show that they were having more and more marital problems and that there was talk of separation again. However, for the time being, Mum seemed to think that they were 'trying'.

All of this is like looking at a bowl of spaghetti and trying to work out which strand ends up in which place. Getting a timeline is hard. One of the issues a lot of survivors have is that when their brain closes down traumatic events, it also closes down good ones. You lose so much. When I've gone back and researched things like music from the seventies and eighties, trying to get a timeline, more memories have come up for me.

When Mum and Dad were together, it came across that she was a really cold woman, but she did have a lot of mental health issues going on – to put it in context, I do have to think about that. Maybe she just couldn't have been a better mum because of that. Dad? Well, I loved him to pieces and he was so funny, but he was a sod to her. When the Birmingham pub bombings happened in 1974, he had gone out and she stayed up all night, thinking he had been killed as it had happened in the very pubs he went to. Dad was missing all night and she was terrified. He rolled in the next morning, having spent all night with one of his women.

'Well, if I wasn't so naughty, I might be dead now!' he told her. 'It was keeping out of that pub and being busy somewhere else that saved me.' He thought it was hilarious. He was a bugger, he really was. He'd always told me that my name was from one of his distant aunts and she'd helped his family when they had money troubles. That turned out to be another one of his stories as it was actually the name of a barmaid that he fancied when Mum was pregnant! He did put her through it, I recognise that. He was a real charmer and he got away with so much.

When we moved to Aston, Dad kept ferrets and he took me ferreting with him, catching rabbits. I loved going out with him but hated the killing of the rabbits. He'd make rabbit stew that was so awful – and *Watership Down* was around at that time too, which made it even worse. Mum never did anything enjoyable with me though. If I was ill, it was Dad who would care for me, or take me to the doctor, or to hospital when I fell off my bike.

That house backed onto a park with a big football pitch that he sometimes took me to for a kickabout. We had a back garden, which was a novelty, and the ferrets had their cage there. Dad was always collecting things. I remember walking to the factory where he worked as a welder one day, my brother in the pram and me toddling along at the side, and coming back with a goat. He'd told Mum to pick it up from someone he worked with as it seemed a good idea to him and she had to walk back with the goat at the side of her too! It was pure white, so we named it Snowy. That went in the back garden too and we had to feed it with a bottle. It was lovely, even if it did chase the dog up the garden and headbutt it. I adored that goat and would spend hours cuddling it.

Some awful children would torment it through the fence though and feed it stones because it would eat anything, which eventually killed it.

* * *

'Come on, Della,' Dad said to me one day, 'let's go on a visit.'

I put my arms into the coat he was holding out for me. 'Where are we going, Dad?' I asked, excitedly. Mum never took me anywhere fun, I was pretty much left to my own devices, but as I've said earlier, Dad was kinder, more engaged. We walked to a nearby block of flats in Newtown and took the lift up to what must have been very close to the top floor. He knocked on a door and when it opened, a glamorous woman with long brunette hair wrapped her arms around him. She kissed my dad for an embarrassingly long time while I stood there scuffing my feet on the ground before, laughing, she said, 'Let's get this little one inside, Arthur!'

I could tell from the moment I walked in that her flat was lovely. It smelled like a florist shop and there were pretty things everywhere. 'This is Debbie,' said Dad to me. 'And this is Della,' he told her.

'I've heard lots about you!' Debbie said, smiling. Dad looked at her as if to say *what are you talking about?* but I didn't care if she was telling the truth at all. I was in a nice place with a nice lady. Maybe she shouldn't have been kissing Dad, I wasn't sure – the important things were the cakes and pop she had for me and the fact that I felt safe when she and Dad left for another room. It turned out that Debbie was an Avon lady and she gave me little samples of perfume and a comb to take home. She was so tickled by my grateful response that she said, 'Let's see what else I can find for you. Maybe something even more grown-up!'

She returned from another room with a full-sized bottle of perfume, the bottle shaped like a lady, which was the most beautiful thing I'd ever owned. When we got home, I couldn't wait to show Mum.

'Look!' I squeaked. 'We've been to see Daddy's friend and she gave me all of this!'

'Daddy's friend?' she asked. 'Daddy's friend? Well, isn't that bloody lovely?'

I remember Dad just looking at her and turning on his heels to walk out of the door. I was left with Mum looking daggers at me. 'Do you remember where this friend lived?' she enquired, very politely, quite calm.

I nodded. She wasn't far away and I knew which tower block we had gone to.

'Let's go pay a visit to her then.' She grabbed me by the wrist before I even had the chance to take my coat off and marched me out of the door. Dad was nowhere to be seen, but I didn't need directions, I could show Mum where Debbie lived and maybe she'd get some nice perfume too. It didn't take long for her to start ranting about Dad and Debbie, and it was clear we weren't going for a social visit. She sounded really cross and I suppose had guessed that they must have been kissing. I was upset about getting Dad into trouble and about spoiling the lovely time at Debbie's.

When we got to the flats she demanded that I take her to 'the floozie'. We got out of the lift and she wanted to know which direction to turn, which door it was. I had no idea and was getting more and more emotional, feeling I'd got everyone in trouble.

'You're absolutely useless,' she told me. 'Always. I can't rely on you for anything. Right, back home.' We got back to her house and she marched into the kitchen and grabbed a carving knife. Throwing the door open, she ran out – back to the flats, I assume – but she mustn't have found Debbie as it wasn't long before Mum slunk back and went to her bed.

Before too long, I heard the door opening, slamming against the wall as the sound of my dad bellowing carried through the whole house.

'What was that about, Carol?' he yelled. 'What the fuck was that about?'

'Now, now, Arthur,' came another voice. 'It's all fine, everything's fine – don't wake up little Della.'

It was Debbie, trying to smooth things over as Mum – now out of bed – and Dad screamed at each other. It went on for a while as I lay there with my hands over my ears, trying desperately to imagine the spaceship dials on my wall. They were hard to find that night – the night Dad moved out to live with Debbie.

There didn't seem to be a broken heart on Mum's side. In fact, it wasn't long before she had a divorce party to celebrate. It was so confusing. One minute she was distraught, with a carving knife in her hand, the next, there was a party going on. She always had a lot of people hanging around and they were all in the house that night, all the friends of hers that I had seen before.

But so too was someone else. Someone new.

Terry Price.

He arrived the night of the divorce party and never left.

* * *

Terry was younger than Mum. He was only 17 when he first entered my life and Mum always said from that point on, whenever she was asked, that she felt sorry for him. Feeling sorry for him was why he became part of our lives.

The living room was full of people, smoke heavy

in the air and music blasting out. There was booze everywhere – which was Mum's focus really – and she didn't waste any effort on the food, more than I had ever seen before in our house. Any time Mum had a party, all of the kids would be put in my room at the top of the house. This was a bigger party than ever before, but that rule still stood. We were all sent upstairs under strict warnings not to come down unless it was a matter of life or death.

Whether it was self-appointed, I don't know, but Terry decided he would be the one checking on us – especially six-year-old me. There were about six kids there that night, bouncing on the bed and dancing about to the music that was blaring up from the room downstairs.

Terry didn't waste much time in getting there and he didn't waste much time in focusing on me.

'Look at you dancing!' he exclaimed. 'You're really good at that, aren't you? You're a great little mover. It's Della, isn't it? Look at you go, Della!'

I never got much attention – well, nothing from Mum – and his words worked perfectly. I kept dancing, kept performing, as he clapped and encouraged me: 'You're a little superstar, aren't you, Della? A little superstar.' I remember him saying those words, I remember that. 'What a princess, what an absolute princess,' he smiled. It all felt very natural, to be honest, he was being nice and I saw nothing bad in that – why would I? He was fun, he was attentive and he started dancing with me too.

'My name's Terry,' he murmured in my ear as he bent down while we danced. 'You'll remember that?'

I nodded, smiling. 'Terry,' I confirmed.

There was no way I'd ever forget that name.

5

DESPERATE

I was so starved of attention from Mum that I was easy pickings for Terry Price. Why wouldn't I be desperate? The fact that I was the only one he was calling a princess, the only one who he said was a great dancer, made it even more special for me. He was there for hours until the party fizzled out. He definitely seemed like a good guy, someone who was non-threatening and made me feel as if I was a talented, lovely little girl.

If this was a film, the audience would be feeling shivers at this point. I do too when I think about it. *Here comes the bad man, here comes the darkness and the terror.* But I only think that way in retrospect, I only know that there should be a pause and the screen should light up with the words, WATCH OUT, DELLA! That first night, I felt good. That night he appeared, I felt seen. *Here he is, into my room and into my life –* and I was completely oblivious. If I could go back and talk to that little girl, I have no idea what I would say. Would I tell her that she would get through this, that she would survive? I don't know. If I did that, I would have to open her up to knowing what was coming and who would want that? If there is something terrible marching towards you, would you want to know what it is, how long it will last for and what it will do to you? I can't really answer that. I know now that I survived, obviously, but there were plenty of times when Terry Price was in my life that I wondered what the ending to my story would be and whether I would be there to see it. He was kind and he was a monster. He was just what I needed and he was the worst thing that could have happened to me.

I got up the next morning and the living room was full of bodies, there were overflowing ashtrays and empty cans everywhere. There was a stench in the air which was a combination of all of it and it seeped through the whole house. Terry was still there and I was pleased about that, hoping when he woke up, I'd have someone be nice to me again.

Already I felt that he was there for me, it was as quick as that.

'Morning, Della,' he said, yawning. 'You come to say hello to your pal Terry, have you?'

I nodded shyly. It felt good that he was saying he was my friend – I needed one of those.

'That was a great night, wasn't it?' he asked.

I nodded again. It had been a great night for me because Terry had been so nice. I remembered all his compliments and when he mentioned my dancing, I felt as if he could read my mind.

'Here, you were a smashing little mover last night! Do you think you'll dance for me again?' When I nodded for the third time, Terry laughed. 'Is that all you can do? Little nodding dog? Well, Princess, don't you worry, you'll soon know that you can say anything to me.'

He lay down again and pulled the cover over him, while I trotted back to my room. It was as sparse as ever, but there was a warm glow inside me that I had something new, I had Terry. I hoped that I would see him again and that he wouldn't be one of the many fleeting men who came in and out of my life. It took me a little while to realise that he had actually moved in and I was never sure whether he and Mum had a relationship. Everything about her life was about the next man and that makes it unlikely they weren't involved sexually. She was always looking for something in the wrong places, but I can honestly say that I never caught them having sex, so I truly don't know. I do know that, despite her being a terrible mother, she constantly looked for people to save – she just didn't look close to home. There is the chance that she was just doing Terry a good turn by letting him move in as it would turn out that he was down on his luck – all through his own behaviour and terrible actions.

Terry did make some things more normal. He cooked, he chatted to me, he even cleaned out the litter trays and played with the cats, which was something Mum never, ever did. She started working in a chip shop, which left Terry as my main carer – she had a live-in babysitter and could now go out whenever she liked.

When she went, if I wasn't trying to stop her – which never worked – at least I had Terry. 'Pop the telly on, Della,' he'd say. 'Let's see if there's something on for you to have a bit of a dance to.' Nothing on TV? 'Pop a record on, Della,' would be his next suggestion. 'Let's have a look at some of your moves, yeah?' I loved it. I loved to dance and I loved that he thought it was worthwhile. Mum would sometimes come back and her only response would be, 'Christ, are you prancing about like a bloody show pony again?'

Mum's obsession with getting a black partner hadn't faded – she'd go with any man, but that was her main goal. Jamaican blues clubs were her favourite haunt, or student events, where she would invariably find someone. She was putting on a lot of weight by this point and claimed that her 'curves' were much more appreciated there – it was an argument that had been ongoing since Dad was at home. He was racist, there's no doubt about that, and used to shout at her that she was nothing more than 'black man's meat'.

'You're disgusting, you're bloody obsessed!' he would shout. 'I don't want to even look at you, you're always sniffing round them, always have been.'

'Why do you think that is?' she'd scream back. 'I want a real bloody man, not a pathetic excuse for one like you.'

One day I remember he shouted at her, 'You've never wanted me, have you? You've always been after one of your black boys.'

'Took you long enough to figure out,' she sniped back. 'I hung on for as long as I could when you'd stuck this one in my belly but had to accept leftovers eventually.'

Now that Dad was gone and Terry was around, she could go chasing men whenever she wanted. Mum was always so drunk or high on medication that she couldn't have cared less about what was going on around her. On top of that, she had been playing with my head for such a long time that I didn't know what was up or down, who was good or who was bad. When Terry moved in, it must have been like she'd won the lottery. She could go out every single night and find who she wanted – and, bizarrely, Terry was more of a parent than she'd ever been. I had to get dressed and take myself to school most of the time as she would still be in bed, drunk from the night before. Pathetically, I still wanted her – I still wanted her to be the mum she never was and never would be.

On the few occasions she did walk me to school, I would strip off on the way – I'd start with my shoes and socks, then the rest of my clothes, scattering them behind me in the hope that it would mean I didn't have to go, I could just go home and be with her all day. It never worked; she'd just drag me there. It's such an odd thing. She was hopeless and completely unloving to me, but I craved her with a fierce intensity and wanted to be beside her constantly. I became known as a naughty child from such an early age because of those behaviours and she certainly wasn't shy about telling people.

'Like a bloody limpet, this one,' she would moan. 'Never off me, clinging on for dear life. I've got to shake her off or she'd never let me get anything done.' She meant that if I was with her, she'd have her wings clipped. She wasn't aiming for a fancy career or anything like that, she just wanted to pick up men.

Mum would go out and Terry would babysit, yet I

would still want to be with her even though he was just being nice to me at that stage. I'd scream while I chased her down the road, begging her to stay at home with me, and she'd just totter along on her high heels, telling me to piss off back home. Did I have a forewarning of what Terry was going to do, is that why I wanted her to stay? I wouldn't have known the words or even known what abuse was, but maybe I sensed that I needed to have someone else there, I needed my mum, in the hope that I would be safe.

Terry was good though – at that point. However, despite being young and tall and slim, he always, always smelled awful. He was never clean and that made me shrink away from him sometimes when he came near. Thinking of him now as he was then, a 17-year-old, he must have never felt that he needed to impress anyone. I didn't get the sense that he ever washed.

Terry didn't work as such, but he sometimes did little jobs as part of his criminal rehabilitation requirements and this was because he was already an offender. He was a convicted sex offender by the time he came into our lives and that, I would think, is why Mum wanted to save him. He was under 17 when he had been caught abusing girls in the care home where he was placed, but because of his age, he had pretty much got away with it.

And he was going to get away with a whole lot more.

It never crossed my mind that he was anything other than a nice man – and he was a man to me, even though he was only 17 at that point. When I went out in the morning, he was there, when I got back, he was there, every weekend he was there. I looked forward to his words, the constant reiteration of how good I was at dancing, of how I was his little princess, of what a superstar he could see I was. What many people don't understand is that the process of grooming isn't just about sexual behaviours, it isn't just when they first touch you inappropriately to see how much they can get away with and what your barriers are before they take it so much further. No, grooming comes from that moment when they are your friend, when they are your only kind person, when they are your caregiver or babysitter. If he washed a bit of dirt off my face, it was part of the grooming. When he said something nice or even winked at me after Mum had kicked off, that was part of the grooming. Even the fact that he cleaned out the cat litter trays meant that my living space was slightly better, slightly less smelly, and that made me think of him in a generous way. All of these things add up and all of it makes you think, *he's nice, I can trust him*. The walls were slowly being broken down, brick by brick, piece by piece.

That is why it has to be up to others to see and act on why these people are inserting themselves into the lives of children. Can that be hard to do? Of course it can – they're clever, they manipulate and they do it gradually. But the facts of the matter were hardly subtle here. I was a little girl known to Social Services who knew what my mother was like. He was an offender who had already been known as a sexual abuser of young girls. And did they do anything? No, no, they did not. They closed their eyes even when they knew he was living with us, and by doing that, they gave him the freedom to do whatever he wanted.

6

'SUCH A PRETTY LITTLE THING'

I was six when Terry first did something which would be part of what was to define my childhood and although I couldn't say exactly how long he had been with us, it felt quick. I think it would have been about three months in, but it's hard to put specific timescales on things from childhood. He was so nice to me but I know now he was actually grooming me from the very first evening of the divorce party. It was as if Dad had gone out one door and he had come in another. All I heard from Terry was that I was a princess, a good girl, a pretty girl.

The bathroom in our house was right next to my mum's bedroom and it was a really bright space as we had a skylight in there. One day, Terry called me in.

'Della, look! Look!' he shouted.

I ran in, expecting to see something exciting, but it

was just him, just Terry standing over the toilet with his hand on his penis.

'Wait until you see this!' he exclaimed. He started moving his hand up and down his penis, getting faster and faster, making more and more sort of groaning noises. All of a sudden, all of this stuff came out of it and he seemed really happy.

'Look at that! There are millions of babies just gone down the toilet there.' In my mixed-up collection of memories, that sticks out. Usually, it all jumbles together and I can try to unravel it and see more of a grooming process, but that has taken time. With what happened in the toilet, I see it very clearly. I couldn't comprehend what he was doing, what was coming out of him or why he was talking about millions of wasted babies. I didn't have any language for so much, but with this, I really did have no clue – I knew what a baby was and I knew that millions was a really big number, but what was he talking about? I didn't know what he was doing but it seemed fantastical. It was something new I'd learned, it was a perverted science lesson. Afterwards it was all normal and he went back to watching telly.

Terry was very good at focusing in on things which interested me, things which caught my attention. I absolutely loved Elvis – he was my hero and I adored all the Teddy Boy stuff that I associated with him. Mum was making me a shiny blue Teddy Girl skirt (a rare attempt at being a good mother) as I wanted to dance around the room to Elvis, with it swirling about round my legs. I used to get so upset when his films were on as I knew Elvis was dead and I would dance to try and cheer myself up. Terry knew how much I loved Elvis and he knew that I loved to dance – which was his way in, complimenting me even more and comforting me when I was crying.

'Ah, don't get upset, Della – come here for a cuddle,' he would say. 'You can still listen to Elvis, you can still watch him on the telly. You're my good girl, aren't you?'

I still adored music and my other favourite thing was *Top of the Pops*. Terry would sit on the sofa while it was on and encourage me to dance even more.

'You're so good, princess, aren't you?' he would exclaim. 'Look at you! Look at you twirling round. Such a pretty little thing – come over here, let me get a better look at you.'

And I would. I would go closer, thinking that he was just admiring my dancing and feeling very proud of how well I was doing in my shiny blue skirt. He was encouraging me to go faster and faster, the skirt getting higher and higher, and although I knew my knickers were showing, I didn't care.

In my memory, things don't really progress slowly. It wasn't terribly gradual, it was as if Terry just decided to do what he wanted extremely quickly. He got me to take all my clothes off very soon. When you have suffered trauma, memories don't behave themselves. They're all over the place, they have a mind of their own inside your own mind. You don't own them, they decide what to do and it can sometimes make no sense. There are gaps too, huge chunks cut out of your own life experiences, and nothing can bring them back. When I think about Terry and when it all began, my memories jump about – there's that, then that, then that, but there are rarely dates or marks in a calendar.

He quickly became keen to talk about what I loved: Elvis and music and dancing. We always had music on so it wouldn't have taken very long to get to that stage of me stripping off. He had complete access to me so neither would it take a while to get where he wanted. Mum was never there. He would be with me when I got home from school, in the evenings and all day at the weekend. It felt like we were playing a game, he made it seem like it was a fun game – twirl round in my skirt and throw it off. He would take his clothes off too so that we were the same, starting with his shirt, then his trousers – and it was all fun, then my skirt, then my top, then my knickers.

I remember watching *Top of the Pops* the first time, which means it must have been a Thursday evening. It was Boney M. on, I know that. Mum was out at a club, which was a regular occurrence now that she had Terry as a live-in babysitter. I was dancing around as I always did, completely lost in the music – and his compliments. They never changed:

You're such a good dancer, Della!

You're so pretty, Della!

Can you spin round for me a bit more, Della?

Look at your little skirt go up! Can you lift it up a bit more for me?

That's really good – why don't you take it off? See if you can dance even better for me?

Why don't you take your top off too?

And your knickers?

Shall I take mine off as well? Keep you company!

So, finally, when he got me naked and dancing, showering all the compliments on me, he was completely naked too. There was a picture in our living room of two children on a swing and they were nude, which made it quite normalised to me. If there were naked people on the wall, where we all sat, then surely it must have been fine? Terry was just doing what they were doing and I was too.

Top of the Pops ended and I was exhausted from all the dancing. And I was happy, I know that. It wasn't a big deal to have no clothes on, he had made it seem quite natural.

'Look at you, all out of breath!' Terry exclaimed. 'Come and sit down on the sofa next to me. Let's have a cuddle.' I'll be completely honest – I was so desperate for the attention that I thought nothing of it, so I did. I gathered up my clothes from the floor, put my pants back on, sat on the sofa with him and let him cuddle me. That sofa is burned in my mind, a dated chocolate brown fabric with lighter brown stripes on it. Before too long, he was kissing me and my pants were off again. Somehow they ended up down the back of the sofa, I don't know how, and we were lying there with him touching me, kissing me and getting me to touch him.

I can't remember it all – I can't remember every single detail. Would I want to? Sometimes. Sometimes I want to know everything that happened, in a neat chronological line. I wonder if that would help, I wonder if having the gaps filled in would give me some sort of closure. Other times, my heart tells me that I can only bear to know so much.

On that night, everything ended really abruptly when Mum came back. Terry rushed me through to my room from the sofa and put me in my bed – we were both naked and he must have heard her key in the door. He had taken my old bedroom when he moved in and I was in the one directly opposite the living room by that point. He threw me onto the bed roughly with my clothes but he mustn't have realised that my pants were still down the back of the sofa. I assume he rushed back and put his clothes on.

By the time Mum came back he would have been doing things to me for a couple of hours. He was making me touch him to the point where he ejaculated. It had been as quick as that. He was blatant as no one was there to stop him and he had complete access to me. I knew no different, but I also didn't know what it all was.

I don't even remember what happened for the rest of that night. I guess I went to sleep – I also guess I was traumatised even if I didn't know it.

The next day Mum found the knickers and I got in so much trouble for leaving dirty pants down the back of the sofa.

'Look at these!' she screamed at me. 'Dirty little bitch! What are you doing, leaving your filthy pants all over the place?'

She questioned nothing. I was six.

When he threw me back in my room that night, the way that he got me to comply with him and not say anything began – and it was that he would promise me things. There was no threat of bad things happening, just the suggestion of good.

'You're a lovely little girl, Della, such a pretty little thing,' he told me. 'I'm going to buy you a present soon.'

I knew exactly what to wish for: there was an Elvis doll in a shop in town, Elvis in a white suit with a microphone which made him sing when you pressed it. I adored it but knew that Mum would never splash out on it for me. I still didn't have toys, so the Elvis doll seemed a complete pipedream, but from the moment Terry knew I loved it, he always promised that he was going to buy me that doll. He dangled it in front of me for so long and I genuinely thought that if I did the things he wanted, I'd get it.

From that one night in front of the TV when *Top of the Pops* was on, he certainly thought nothing of touching me or getting me naked whenever the opportunity arose. He often took me out with him and those trips now included a look at the Elvis doll in the window of the shop selling it. Terry would take me to his probation meetings and we'd look at the doll on the way, as well as going into a pet shop to see a talking parrot that sat on a swing. They were nice things to do. I knew that if I'd said anything, there wouldn't have been the trips to the pet shop and I wouldn't have had a chance of the Elvis doll – that's how he manipulated me.

I never did get the doll.

The thought that a 17-year-old convicted paedophile was taking a little girl to his probation meetings is just horrendous, but no one cared. No one asked questions, no one thought to raise it as suspicious. The thing is, I enjoyed those trips, Terry made them fun. They gave him money at the meetings and he would take me for something to eat in Birmingham city centre afterwards, to the Teddy Boy and Rockers café, buying me sweets when we left to eat on the bus home. It was a nice day out, I was special and he was spoiling me. If I had to do the other things, that was just a trade and I didn't know they were abnormal.

It seems such a failure of duty of care allowing me to be at those probation meetings, but it happened a lot. It was just part of life and was actually something to look forward to. There were even toys at the probation office. It makes me so angry now. They knew that he was a convicted paedophile and that he was living in our home, with access to me. He was under probation for that very reason, yet he was turning up with a child as if flaunting me under their noses! They never spoke to me and I just played. They never asked me how I was, how I knew Terry, why I was with him. Terry didn't seem to care either – he had landed on his feet: he had a woman who wasn't bothered about her kid, he had access to me, she was out all the time, leaving him in sole care and even the authorities turned a blind eye. There were two occasions in the records where the Probation Service wrote to Social Services to ask what was going on, but there was no follow up.

Terry Price had committed crime after crime, with no gaps in between. He was a prolific offender. Even when he was with us, he was done for another rape. He didn't give up, he was acting against the law constantly and yet it was all seen as almost forgivable. Apparently, he was abused himself as a child. I don't know if that's true, but it's no excuse. The vast majority of those who were abused as children grow up to be good, kind people who never hurt children and it's an insult to them to suggest that abuse committed against them in childhood makes them go on to become a paedophile.

It's awful to say, but Terry was nice to me – for those memories, there is no nastiness. He knew what he was doing. There were other instances that my mind just won't go to, it comes out in night terrors and flashbacks with no control. When I say he was nice though, I mean the way he was with me, the compliments and making me feel special. As I said before, physically he was actually repulsive. He was dirty and smelly, he stank of BO and stale cigarette smoke. One of the most prominent things about him was his mouth – it was very flat and he had horrible teeth. He was thin as a rake and I could feel his bones whenever he hugged me. He was disgusting – but he was also all I had. Terry had quite a strong Scottish accent but I don't know exactly where he was from. When he was in care, he had been in Scotland and then came to England afterwards. I later realised this was a deliberate pattern of his – he would get caught, then move to somewhere else. He was no fool, but he managed to fool practically everyone.

I get so frustrated that I can't remember things in their entirety. As an adult, I understand how the brain works and how it protects you, but in the same breath it isn't really helpful, as I would like to remember it all so that I can file it away. I can't process what I went through properly and so it's constantly replaying in my mind. It's like only getting certain scenes from a film rather than the whole of it, so I can't make sense of the story. There is more narrative my brain holds, but my mind is protecting me. I would rather know it all though, I think. I know there are more horrors to be found, but imagining what they might be is almost as bad as knowing.

7

WISHES

Sexual abuse is so often a process with many stages. I know that there were stages with Terry Price, but in my mind, those memories don't follow the stages – it's like a puzzle I have to piece together in my head. I do know that after the incident when I was watching *Top of the Pops,* he just assumed that I would get naked whenever he asked. To be honest, it became normalised for me too. I was young, only six, and my whole life up to that point had been dysfunctional anyway. The only other life I had seen was that of Carolyn when she took me to her home. That was unusual in my world though, which made the normality of it seem almost off. It was a completely topsy-turvy way of living and thinking. A dad in prison, being left alone in a flat since I was a tiny little thing, Mum neglecting me, in and out of care, my parents splitting up over and over again, Terry abusing me – *that* was normal.

The abuse, the constancy of the abuse, was initially around him touching me and getting me to touch him.

'Go on,' he would say to me, 'touch it, touch it.'

I didn't have the words for what he was getting me to do or what he was wanting me to touch, but whenever he did get me to fondle his penis, it was always with him still telling me how good I was. The touching became more and more frequent, and he started to give me instructions.

'No, not like that, don't stop, Princess,' he'd encourage. 'Keep going, move your hand up and down, that's a good girl.'

'It hurts, it hurts my hand,' I'd tell him.

'No, no, it doesn't – just keep going.'

I was completely bewildered the first time 'something' happened when I moved my hand about. Why did his thing get so much bigger and then why did he start making a sort of groaning noise? I worried that I was hurting Terry but he seemed very keen that I keep going. He would make such noises and I couldn't work out why he wanted it to go on. Then, all of a sudden, the 'something' happened. I had no idea what it was. A pouring out from his thing, warm, sticky stuff like glue.

He seemed very pleased with it as he stopped making all of those awful noises once it came out and he kept saying, 'That's it, that's it, good girl, good girl, Della.'

I didn't have the vocabulary or the knowledge of any of this. Did millions of babies always come out when it happened? I didn't know what it meant for a man to ejaculate, I didn't know what a hand job was – I didn't know what abuse was. All I knew was that I was a good girl and I was Terry's princess.

In my mind, these memories don't come in steps or stages, it's just one big muddle of awful stuff that was done to me.

My mum's bedroom was one of my favourite places in my very small world. In the living room, we had a long cupboard with a radiogram in. You lifted up the top of the cupboard and this massive record player was inside. In Mum's bedroom was a smaller version. She had a big stack of records there too and I would sneak in when I got a chance and put one on so that I could dance around the room to my heart's content, listening to everything from Tammy Wynette and Dolly Parton to the reggae which Mum favoured above everything else. I felt safe in there, which makes me wonder whether there was a part of me that knew dancing in front of Terry would lead to things that weren't right.

Mum had a double bed with a duvet on it – duvets were quite modern back then, most people had winceyette sheets and scratchy blankets. However, Mum had made herself a lovely little oasis, with a deep blue duvet cover she had stitched by hand. She enjoyed sewing and stitching, and it was a good way to save money. She had a bedside lamp made of frosted glass with a blue moon on it and there were nice things everywhere. Little ceramic ornaments of birds were all round her room, a collection she was really proud of, and in complete contrast to the fact that I didn't really have anything personal in my room at all. There were lots of perfumes and make-up lying around too as she was a big fan of Avon (despite the memories of Debbie) and used to go to parties when any of her friends were selling things. Mum's room was a lot more comfortable than mine in every way and it became a refuge for me.

I felt safe there, but Terry broke that.

That was my little place to dance but he ruined it, he took that haven from me and turned it into somewhere full of bad memories. I was lying on Mum's bed one evening while she was out, as usual. I was daydreaming, looking at all the little bird ornaments and wishing I could have something like that in my room.

The door opened and Terry walked in.

'What you up to, Princess?' he asked. 'Why are you in here all alone?' I couldn't answer him – I knew I didn't want to be in the living room with him, but I couldn't really bring my thoughts together. 'Why don't I join you?' he said, but it was a statement not a question. 'You like it in here, don't you?' he reflected, looking around. 'Pop your clothes off like a good girl, why don't you?'

I did what he wanted – I always did.

Mum used to smoke and there were always fags and matches everywhere in the house, including on the cabinet at the side of her bed. I don't know how the next bit happened but, somehow, somehow, he got me to put matchsticks into my vagina. I need to get across to you now that a traumatised mind doesn't work as cleanly as people might hope. Flashbacks go *bump, bump, bump* in your head and you don't necessarily know how you got to a place or point, you just know that you did. It isn't a nice and neat timeline, it doesn't work like that. I just remember lying on the bed and he had me with my knees up and was telling me to put them in. So I did. He made it into a game; he had gained my trust and was a fun person to be around, given that I had no attention from any other adult.

The matchstick episode was early on, as was him masturbating in the bathroom and showing me what had come out of him. I had no idea what it was, I was so little that we hadn't done anything like sex education at school.

School wasn't really any sort of release for me either – I always tried to escape and get back to Mum. This isn't the sort of story like Matilda, where there is a lovely Miss Honey to get me out of it all. I was just a little girl without the words to describe or make sense of what was going on. I couldn't tell anyone what was happening as I didn't know what it was, but I did slowly start to know that I didn't want to be alone with Terry. If Mum wasn't there, he'd do 'things' to me, even if I couldn't describe what those things were.

When I was at school, I knew Mum was at home as it was daytime and I desperately wanted to get back to her, even if she didn't want me. She would take me in one gate, I'd go to a planned lesson and then just try to escape round the other side of the school. I'd have to go on my hands and knees to get past the headmaster's office. In my little brown duffle coat, I would sneak past below his window to get out of the school gate again. He used to sometimes talk to the kids about the brown dog that was in the school playground and warn them not to let their pets follow them to school, but it was me!

If Terry wasn't looking after me, he would be out doing his own thing and those were the times I craved. Despite everything with Mum, she was still my safety net, she was the one I wanted to be with – did I think if she knew about the abuse, she would stop it? I don't really know, it was more of a gut feeling than that, a feeling of life being better when she was around. When

I did manage to escape and get back to her, on the times I did get home, the 'wag' woman would come out – she would have been called by the school liaison officer by now – sometimes having to chase me over the fields as I would be running from her. When I did get home on those few times, Mum would always be in bed. She'd be so angry with me that I would wonder why I had bothered.

On nights when she went out, I would be screaming, hanging onto her legs.

'I need a break from you!' she'd yell. 'You're a bloody nightmare, you never leave me alone. I need some time on my own – get off me!'

Even though she was the safest person in my world, she didn't give me anything to actually make me feel warm or loved. As an adult, I've been a single mum myself and it's hard, it's really hard, and you do need a break sometimes. But when you have a child that is obviously so desperate for you, not just missing you a little bit, how can you ignore it, how can you not question why? I'd be screaming, begging, and rather than thinking I'm just a naughty child, you need to ask why that child is doing that. I have made a lot of excuses for her over the years – yes, she was brought up in care, yes, she had no one who really showed her how to be a good mum, but the older I get and the more knowledgeable I am, I know it's just an excuse. I haven't had a role model but I've managed and I would never let anyone lay a finger on my kids. The one gift she gave me was lessons in how not to be a mum.

Mum had lots of one-night stands at this point because now she had a constant babysitter who always seemed more than happy to look after the little girl she found so irksome. Terry freed her up to do whatever she wanted, but I guess there must have been occasions when he wasn't there and she worried about having her wings clipped again. For my mother, I wasn't an excuse to stay at home rather than go out chasing men – no, her reasoning was that I could go along with her. Once, she took me to Portsmouth. It felt so exciting and she bought me a book for the journey. It was a rhyming one:

> *Star light, star bright*
> *First star I see tonight.*
> *I wish I may, I wish I might,*
> *Have this wish I wish tonight.*

I hung onto those words for a long time. That day, on that trip, I honestly thought we were just having a lovely day out. You used to get little bars of chocolate at the train station vending machine and that all added to the feeling that we were going on a trip. She had this thing for Nigerian men that I mentioned before and we were actually going to students' accommodation to meet one of them. When I got there, I was just put in front of the TV and left. On this occasion she even let one of them give me a bath. I remember that he had this massive loofah thing, the likes of which I'd never seen in my life, and here was this strange, huge man who was scrubbing me. He didn't do anything untoward, but what on earth was going through Mum's mind? She'd had sex while I watched telly, then she lay there, during the day, while he came out of the room and bathed me. We stayed overnight that time.

Once, she took me to London to meet a man and while she was with him, I got kicked out to wander about on my own while she was up there with him. 'Just go to the park,' she told me. I was only eight and I was being told to walk around London on my own while she had sex. I was just dumped. Another time she took me to Birmingham to a university there, and while she was in the room with whoever it was, she let one of the other blokes take me out, as if that was all fine. We went round and he showed me the sports hall and suchlike, but then he put his arm around me and tried to pull me in to kiss me in the lift. I had to push him off until the lift got to the right floor and then I ran out. She put me in so many vulnerable positions and just didn't care. I don't know how she contacted all these men, there was no social media back then. It was a lot of organisation but she must have liked the thrill of it all as it seemed such a lot of bother to make so much effort. I can hardly believe that she did those things, but they're seared into my mind and I actually think I was lucky that more didn't happen to me.

It's funny what you think of as 'lucky' when you're raised in a world like that.

8

NICE THINGS

I was such a little thing and Terry was a grown man – I don't think that really hits you until you're an adult too. The actual terrifying nature of having someone that size, in all senses, telling you what to do. I remember him lying on Mum's bed naked so many times and just assuming that I would do as I was told, that I would get naked too. He was quite right to assume that, as I always did.

It did progress but it was always within the context of him being nice to me at that stage. He never threatened me or made me feel scared, he just made me feel as if it was a natural thing which happened with the person who looked after you. Deep down, I must have felt something was off due to the number of times I chased after Mum, not wanting to be left alone with Terry, but there was nothing which would have made me verbalise it.

'Do you want me to do something nice to you,

Della?' he asked one night. We were on Mum's bed as usual and she was out somewhere, maybe working at the chippy as she still did a few shifts there.

I nodded. I would really like to dance about or maybe make up a game that we could play that didn't involve us having no clothes on.

'Good girl, good girl!' Terry said, but as I went to get off the bed, he pushed me back down. 'Where d'you think you're going? Lie there, we're going to do nice things together.'

I couldn't imagine what we could play while we were in bed like that, but I really hoped it would be something good. After very little time, I got a funny feeling. Terry was at my private parts but not with his hand, which was what he usually did. It felt like he was kissing me down there. I just lay there while he kept doing it, then he sort of manoeuvred me and said that I could do something lovely for him too.

He had pushed and pulled me down the bed so that my head was close to his genitals. 'We can feel nice together,' he murmured, as he shoved my head into him. My bottom was still up towards him and he was still trying to kiss me there. It was traumatic for me because it smelled disgusting and I felt like I was going to be sick – I still have a really bad gag reflex now – but I was getting really upset because there was a feeling like I was going to wet myself. I kept telling him as I was scared, I knew I would get in trouble, but Terry said, 'It's fine, carry on.'

I'm so ashamed to write this, but I have to.

That was probably the first orgasm I had and now, as an adult, processing that, it makes me sick. How dare he take that away from me? I know that it was only my body reacting normally, but I hate it. I hate that he made me go through that and gave me that as a memory. I feel like my body betrayed me at that time. As an adult who has experienced abuse, you end up with this horrible connection between normal things that you should enjoy and the memory of when that happened to you as a child. You think you must have enjoyed it if that happened, you must have been asking for it.

He ejaculated then too, with him on his side next to me. It was disgusting, *he* was disgusting, but he had broken down that barrier now too and it was just part of the abuse repertoire.

It could happen any time – weekends, after school, evenings, any moment that Mum wasn't there, just whenever he chose to abuse the access to me that he had. She'd be at work or going out to clubs or meeting up with men, and he would see his moment. They both gained a lot from it – her life was open and he had a child to abuse on tap.

At some point in my files, there is a report which says my nan had concerns. I had run away to her house on one occasion when I couldn't bear being around Mum any longer. She lived about two miles away and I loved her house, spending as much time there as I could. She wasn't my blood nan, just stepmother to Mum, but I loved her to bits. She is where I got my maternal side from. There are times I remember where we planted things in her garden together, and she did huge curries and fed anyone who came round; she was more motherly than Mum by a million miles. I'd never have told her though. She was tough and had brought up a lot of kids on her own, but she wouldn't have a bad word said about her sons, mum's step-brothers, which is why I knew she'd never believe me.

No matter what her boys did, they were right – even when three of them got done for armed robbery! She would protect them to death. Nobody would dare say a bad word about them. The boys would bring her things back that they had robbed, always give her money, and she sat at the centre of the family like an absolute matriarch. Maybe Mum got her notion to collect waifs and strays from her as she was another one who would take anyone in.

Nan had a weekly ritual of going shopping on a Saturday and anyone who was around was dragged off with her. Most people tried to avoid these 'shopping' trips as one thing would go in her trolley and another would be stuffed up her jumper. Mum told me of one time when she was heavily pregnant with me that Nan got caught shoplifting and she was so embarrassed, being carted off to the police station with Nan and a huge belly. Was this another of Mum's stories, though? I'll never know, but it would fit with what I knew of Nan!

One weekend, I was left with a friend of the family while mine went off to the shops. He was always only too keen to offer to babysit. He asked me to play a game, but it was a set-up. I can't actually work out whether that was the first time I was abused, or whether Terry was first, as it was around the same time. All I know is that there was a point where he was touching me, then …

Blackout.

When I came to, I was screaming. His hand was over my mouth, the stench of sweat in my nose, as he whispered frantically, 'Keep quiet, keep quiet! Don't say anything and I'll take you out next week.'

There was no trip out.

I know that he went on to abuse others. I used to always volunteer to babysit any kids we knew from about the age of 11 as I felt that was the only way they would definitely be safe. A family riddled with abuse was the dynamic wherever I looked. I need to find a way to understand that now. I couldn't then, but when abuse starts at such a young age, it programmes the child. If you aren't getting affection from anywhere else, you look for it everywhere. If someone shows you the slightest bit of attention or affection, it has a totally disproportionate effect and opens you up to thinking, maybe they will be a nice person, the person that you need. When the abuse starts and escalates, you're already primed to play it down because you need something from them. Care, attention, love – they feed the basic needs of a child. Abusers meet those needs and they know that, they sense the vulnerability like an animal smelling blood.

So many people know these men and we need to face up to that. Children are given these messages so often – stay away from *them*, don't sit on *their* lap – but we fail to unpack what is behind that. We put it all on the child, it's *their* responsibility to not go near them or be in a room alone with them. If the child doesn't stick to the rules they were given, it's their fault. It's twisted. There isn't any other crime that is dealt with like that. Why is there so much effort put into hiding it and justifying the abusers while blaming the victims?

It's because the world would be split open if we ever faced up to the extent of paedophilia.

Families don't want to air their 'dirty laundry' in public and that perpetuates the notion that it's shameful – but it's the child who carries the shame, not the abuser. They carry it for life and we need to change that. That's what drives me now and it's the only way I can make sense of what happened then.

I can only describe the two years between 1979 and 1981 as a reign of terror, really. Every day, I woke up wondering what Terry Price would do next. I was still chasing after Mum whenever she would leave me with him. I knew what was coming, but she just thought I was being naughty and it was even more reason to get away from me – I was uncontrollable. I didn't know how to tell her what he was doing to me. If you see a child in such distress, and they are only like that when a particular person is looking after them, why wouldn't you ask questions? She didn't care. I would just go back into the house once the taxi had gone away, and often, he'd be there, watching me look as my mum left, taking me back in to the house.

'Come on in, we'll watch the telly, we'll play some music,' he would say, but that wasn't what he meant. That wasn't what we were going to do at all.

I do have one or two good memories in the middle of everything in those years. There used to be a Saturday morning show on Central Television with a character called Metal Mickey – I was desperate to meet him. I wrote in and me and my brother got to go on! We were taken into the studio waiting area where Spike Milligan came in, who played the character.

'Can I have your autograph?' I asked him.

'I don't do those,' he said, 'but you can have this.' He handed me a manky plaster off his finger. 'There you go, aren't you lucky?'

There was a competition for all of us and at the start, they said, 'Whoever dances the best will get a prize at the end.' By then, I wasn't dancing any more. That had gone for me. I remember standing there, glaring, as my brother did all his best Shakin' Stevens moves. The cameras were fixed on him, but they were also showing his furious sister, who was thinking he was showing her up! I was mortally embarrassed by him. But it was a really good day and I hold onto those, because there are so few of them.

9

TERROR

Of course Terry started to rape me, of course he did. Why wouldn't he? What was there to stop him?

I don't know when it happened for the first time. All I really recall from some point is the sensation of a cushion pressing behind me – I guess as my head sank into it from the weight of Terry on top – and of not being able to move.

And the pain, always the pain.

I couldn't understand why he would want to put that thing inside me. The excruciating pain every time would shoot through me – how could it not? How could a small child's body get used to a grown man doing that to her? He would move about, thrusting inside of me for what seemed like a long time, then there would come a groan from him and I would feel a disgusting wetness drip down my legs. I knew that it was the stuff which held the million babies, the stuff he had shown me go down the toilet and I had seen so many times when I had given him hand jobs. The thought of that inside my body made me sick.

Terry would try and lie there on top of me for a bit while he recovered. Again, the weight of him was intolerable and I would try and get to the toilet as quickly as I could. I'd wipe myself with a wad of toilet paper or with a facecloth but was always worried that the stench of what came out of him would alert Mum. Why did I worry about that? I suppose I thought I would be the one to get into trouble. She seemed to like Terry but she didn't like me, I was just a nuisance.

Terry would do all the usual things like telling me what a good girl I was, saying that we'd had a nice time together, but I couldn't pretend. I would just want him to leave me alone. Often when I sat down afterwards, I would get shooting pains and I constantly thought back to how I thought I would die when he was crushing me. I probably did black out sometimes as he was close to suffocating me. I couldn't breathe, my chest felt like it would collapse when he was on top of me. I want to make sense of this, I want all of this to be contextualised so that people understand and don't think I'm making this up, but it all merges into one. He raped me and I can't give you any more details than I have.

In 1980, my Great Nan died. She was the lovely, homely, caring Nan that I loved so much, so I assumed that I would go to the funeral. I felt that I was a big girl now, but, more importantly, I didn't want to be left alone with Terry in case he did 'those' things.

'No, you're not coming,' Mum announced. 'Why would you?'

'I just want to,' I told her.

'That's a stupid reason, it's not a reason at all. You're just a kid. Stay here – don't worry, Terry will be with you.'

I became really upset, crying, begging her to let me go, but she was adamant. On the day of the funeral – which must have been during school holidays, or maybe I was just bunking off – she set off in the morning with barely a backwards glance.

'I'm going to a bloody funeral,' she snapped. 'I can do without your whining.'

'Don't worry, Carol,' Terry assured her. 'We'll have a great time, won't we, Della?' I ignored him. 'Princess? I'm saying that we'll have a great time while Mum's out, won't we?'

I stormed up to my room. There was no point chasing after Mum or clinging to her leg. This wasn't a decision she'd change, I'd just get a whack around the head and a mouthful of cursing. I know that Terry stayed downstairs for a while and that I was lying on Mum's bed when it happened.

I remember Mum coming back. She'd brought me a pink quilted dressing gown to make up for not letting me go to the funeral.

And before she came back, what happened? A jump. A huge jump.

That day was the first day that Terry anally raped me. He had been getting closer, always touching me around that area, and I couldn't understand why. It was a dirty place. A place that was for other things, it was just for going to the loo, which meant that I couldn't comprehend in the slightest why he would want to put his fingers there. I was always worried that I might have dirt on me rather than that he shouldn't be there in the first place. He'd put his fingers in before, which hurt, but the day of Nan's funeral was different. There's no film reel playing in my mind to give the full story, instead it comes in fits and starts.

Him pushing me over onto my front.

My face being shoved into the bed on top of the quilt.

Thinking I was going to suffocate as he pushed me harder and harder ...

Then the pain. Dear God, the pain.

I'm going to split, I'm going to split in two.

And the words – they changed. I wasn't a princess any longer.

You love this don't you?

You wanted this.

You want it so much.

You dirty little whore, this is what you want.

Horrible things said in a nasty, threatening way. But no step-by-step memory, just him not being in the room, then him being in my mum's room, then the pink dressing gown and the snippets flooding back over the next few days.

I was so traumatised that I wouldn't, couldn't, eat and Mum just put that down to me being upset as I hadn't been allowed to go to the funeral. That wasn't the reason – that wasn't the reason at all. I had no control over my bowels afterwards, absolutely none. I was terrified that Mum would find the pants I kept dirtying and I'd get into trouble. I tried to hide them but the fear that she'd smell something and work out where they were brought me out in a cold sweat. I kept going to the bathroom to wash them out. It was constant.

Most of the flashbacks I have are of being held down once he started raping me like that. They're not like fully formed conscious memories, they're of being held down, of not being able to breathe, of panicking. I couldn't scream as there was no air, not that there would have been anyone to hear me. When he raped me that way, he would be nasty every time, telling me that I deserved it. Before too long, every act of abuse was characterised by that sort of insult. I wasn't a good dancer or a princess any more.

The flashbacks give me snapshots of what he said and what he did. To this day, I can't sleep with a quilt anywhere near my face. I just remember such pain and that I couldn't sit down afterwards. I still get flashbacks of that pain, of the memories. Sometimes they are the most difficult to go through, as they will happen when I'm asleep. I wake up and I can't sleep, tossing and turning, crying out. I get it now where the pain is so intense that I can't sit down. It's horrendous, the flashbacks come out of nowhere and I can't stand up, I can't bend over. That is what Terry Price has done to me for his moments of pleasure.

Smells are another problem, anything which makes me remember being near him and the gagging I would experience. I fully understand as an adult that I made coping mechanisms when I was a child, and that was needed at the time, but it doesn't work for me any longer. I go right back to that time when it happens. There aren't just fight-or-flight responses to trauma, there's becoming frozen as well, which is my main go-to. I've always had blackouts without really knowing what they were, but I have come to understand that they're my body's way of just shutting down. I freeze to such a degree that I black out.

I must have been in distress obviously, but he was always telling me to shut up, saying horrible, nasty things, because he was a completely different person now from the caregiver he had been. Yes, he was still there when Mum wasn't, but there were no nice words or encouragement anymore. Suddenly, he was someone completely different. He had changed into a monster, and his behaviour or words weren't nice or loving any more. As a child, you try to work that out. One minute they are one person, then another, then when it's over, they are back to the first person again. That does your head in. He had put me through so much abuse before but he was 'nice' then. Now, he was horrible and I had so much guilt thinking I would rather go back to the other stuff and the other him.

Once he started raping me anally, that became part of what he wanted to do all the time. From February 1980, from my great-nan's funeral, he knew he could do whatever he wanted without any repercussions. I have no idea how many times it happened – at least until 1981, he was at me all the time because he had free rein.

He would still take me to the shops sometimes, we'd go find sticklebacks down the canal, and there would be more trips to the pet store. But instead of the trips being a promise of love, care and potential gifts and toys, they became psychological torture.

I'm trying to give you the full story here but there are chunks missing, where the awful things are, but I'll do what I can. You don't just lose the trauma, you lose part of your development – you become stunted in a way.

***

Terry's behaviour towards me was totally unbalanced – he'd rape me then revert to being nice again. That was how he played it – not pushing me, I guess. I think he toed that line very well: he made sure I wanted the nice part of him and he was very clued-up. I did fantasise about telling Mum and her having the right reaction. Sometimes I would even mutter things under my breath in the hope she might hear me – she never did.

Mum was still finding ways to use as many people as she could, whether social workers or the many men she was in touch with. She had loads of boyfriends and lots of ways to manipulate them. 'We're going to see Geoff (or Peter or Gary),' she would say. 'As soon as we get there, tell him you need new shoes. I'm not paying for them. You better make a good show of it or you'll get nothing.' If I told her I didn't want to, she'd just reply, 'It's just a game. Stop complaining –

you want shoes, don't you? Well, this is the way to get them. But get money. I'll buy you them later. You hear me? Don't let him say he'll take you for shoes, just get the cash.'

After the coaching, she'd turn on me if I said a word out of place.

'Don't say that! What are you on about? God, how embarrassed do you want me to be?' she'd snap.

Geoff (or Peter or Gary) would often fall for it, consoling Mum that they didn't mind, that children often said things they shouldn't, and she'd simper, playing the embarrassed mum who was so ashamed that her runaway husband had left her penniless. Of course, she only wanted the money for herself, as she'd made clear to me. If they had actually said, 'Right, let's go into town and get you shoes,' she wouldn't have known what to do – keep the receipt and take them back, I guess.

I was just something for them to use, both Terry and Mum got what they wanted out of me and still no one was noticing, still no one was taking me out of that environment.

You never know what's coming with an abuser. Sometimes they don't do bad stuff as they want to keep you in a state of fear – the fact that was done to me at a crucial stage of development means that my brain has been formed that way. With anything difficult now, my body says, that's enough and shuts down. There are also so many triggers. If I pass someone in the supermarket and they smell a certain way, that reminds me of what I've been through. I can't stand someone smoking near me, even though I used to do it myself – a wave goes over me. I see him everywhere I go, even on the telly, in the shops, anyone who looks like him. As I used to have to wash my pants in the bathroom, I now have to clean my bathroom constantly. If I have a shower, I don't just clean it, I have to clean the whole room: sink, toilet, floor, it has to look like I haven't even been in there.

And music? Well, he took that from me, didn't he? I had loved it. It's a particularly challenging trigger as I have no control over if and when I hear it – going to supermarkets is hard, if they play old tunes. It's more likely there, too. Places like the GP surgery, or sometimes hospitals, will have local radio on in the background. (So many health settings aren't trauma informed and don't think about things like that, but when the sounds of the seventies and eighties are blasting out and I'm taken back to 'then', it's difficult to concentrate on anything else.)

10

NO ONE TO BLAME

The social workers knew Terry Price. They made no risk assessment and took no protective action on my behalf. In July 1980, the main social worker assigned to us, Catherine, filed a report which said that she had identified Terry Price at our home address in Aston and simply explained that she was no longer involved in our case as she had suggested no further action (which was granted the day after her report and overseen by a second social worker) due to Mum breaking her contract with them on many occasions. Mum went back on her word and all the things she agreed with the social workers on pretty much every occasion. Even when she did make basic concessions, she was clear that she disagreed and that had been the case for years.

I fully believe that Catherine's lack of action put me at risk with regards to Price. It also set the scene for how I was to be failed by the social work team based in Aston at every point in the future. Regardless of the era and social work practice at that time, there were so many clear signs that I was at risk and that it was being at best minimised, at worst ignored. To have Catherine's report signed off by a second social worker as 'no further action needed' is, in my mind, negligent in terms of duty of care to anyone who spends even a second looking at it.

The previous social work team was very aware of Mum's lack of co-operation but persisted in their duties to provide regular check-ups because they understood the dangers that she posed in leaving me unattended and vulnerable. They were also fully aware of her tendency to overdose. Around the time of her divorce from Dad in 1982, she tried to end her life and I found her unconscious in the bathroom after she had cut her wrists. I raised the alarm with a neighbour who was a nurse and Mum was taken to hospital while the neighbour looked after us. There isn't actually any record of this in my file, therefore no safeguarding follow-up happened either.

Once I was in the house in Aston and attending Aston Towers Junior School, I continually ran away, yet there is little evidence on file of the school and

Social Services working together, as had previously been the case in Nechells. Aston failed from the outset – even with something so obvious as a sex offender living alongside a little girl and her negligent mother.

In 1981, things finally changed.

***

Terry Price was done for manslaughter. He stabbed a man 47 times in an absolute frenzy, but he was only given three years. I didn't have any information about how long he would be in prison, which meant there was no sense of relief that he would be away from me for a certain amount of time. Mum had to start taking me with her pretty much all the time when she went to see other men, but it was something I was used to by then.

This was also a time when I had to become more self-sufficient. Terry had been my main carer and that is a duality I still live with today. You make excuses for people, you look for the human side, in the hope that it can take over. You become forgiving of what they did and remember that they were caring at times. Survivors have their heads messed with so much that they don't know which way is up – you constantly look for the good in people because if you don't have that, what do you have? Terry was gone and I had to step up, look after me and my brother, do the cleaning, do the cooking. I took on that responsibility and had to grow up really fast. I didn't need Mum to tell me – she probably wouldn't have bothered if we were hungry or living in a tip anyway. There were times during the day when she left us, but not so much during the night as when we were toddlers. I became Mum. My brother was still little but, like me, had been used to looking after himself, so he would ask if he could go to the shops alone and my stomach would lurch with the worry that something might happen to him. I knew that if he did go, he'd get distracted and start playing with any friends he met on the way. I didn't have the authority to keep him at home constantly though and had to allow a bit of freedom, although the fear was always there that something awful would happen. I had to become the adult so quickly.

When Terry was in prison, Mum had so many men coming round to her house that I'm sure she must have been a prostitute. The amount of men who turned up at our door was unreal and she always had plenty of money for herself, although she'd spend none of it on us and would plead poverty to the social workers. At one point, one of the neighbours even came in regularly and she was definitely having sex with him. She kept saying that I needed to ask men for things too, trying to get even more money. One Asian man, who was training to be a doctor, brought a bag of sweets for me and she later told me that I didn't know how lucky I was as she always told them to bring me something. I got chocolate and even a tin of Danish biscuits from one man.

There were two different student places where she would go, trailing me with her, to see ones she was set up with, one in Handsworth and another in Ladywood. Some she would go to a few times, but there were one-offs too. I liked the man in Ladywood as he would take me to the video shop first to get something to watch and eat while he and my mum were doing what they did. I could always hear her having sex, if she hadn't kicked me out as she did in London, and the student accommodation especially wasn't exactly private.

'What are you looking at?' she'd ask if I even glanced sideways at her. 'Don't you judge me! Don't you blame me for anything! Don't you dare think you know what my life is like!'

Now that Terry was in prison, I did have a feeling that home was safer, I just didn't know how long that would last. I didn't cling to Mum when she left – if I wasn't being dragged along too, I would lock the door and just wait, thankful that I wasn't being abused by him, thankful for the very little I had. There were moments I clung to. She once told me that when I was a baby, she couldn't believe I was hers and that when I started talking, I was 'posh', which she didn't understand. I wanted those stories desperately and asked for them over and over again; they were few and far between, crumbs she threw me to keep me onside. She had that duality too. While never there for me, Mum was really giving and caring to other people – I wanted those bits but they were never something I could keep. Maybe she never formed a bond with me and I often wondered if it was something I lacked that stopped her. If she could be that caring with other people, why not me? Was I the wrong sort of little girl for her?

Two doors away we had a neighbour a little bit older than me, the closest I would get to a best friend, a girl called Sally. We'd sit in the garden making mud pies and we would let our imaginations run away. Her family was awful too, really abusive and the house was bad – even worse than mine. It was on another level of filth: there were dead puppies under newspapers and if you opened the door, you couldn't breathe. Her mum looked like a homeless person with bedraggled hair and one brother treated her like a slave. Mum said Sally could stay with us for a bit and she went over the top with being really good to her. It was all part of wanting to save everyone but not looking under her own nose. She fed Sally, bought her stuff and I became really jealous and fought with her. I didn't have much of my mum anyway and now suddenly she had another little girl, a new toy to spoil. Sally eventually went into foster care and I lost the only friend I had.

I remember sitting crying in front of a mirror in my bedroom and knowing that I wanted to see someone when I was upset. I wanted to be looked after, I didn't want to just cry alone. It is such a bizarre thing to think that the only way I could have some sort of interaction was with my own reflection. I would look at myself crying and somehow try and get something back from me that I didn't get back from Mum. That is a strange thing for a nine-year-old to process and to even come up with in the first place, but it was just one of my coping mechanisms.

I was out a lot, at other people's houses, walking the streets. Now that Terry had gone, I spent a lot of time trying not to be around Mum, the exact opposite to how it had been when he was there. She would give me nothing – why bother ever trying to have a relationship with her?

I still lived in my imagination a lot. There would be a few toys at Christmas, but not much, and nothing that lasted. It was all cheap. I spent ages walking around looking for lollipop sticks. I'd make little houses with my collection, paint them and entertain myself that way. School was awful. I'd had to grow up so quickly and if I saw someone being picked on or bullied, it hit me hard. I always spoke up and the bullies didn't like that. If a little kid was being hit, I'd be right in there, but I got bullied too.

Mum made me wear tights to school one day.

'I'm not wearing those,' I told her. 'They're too old, they're for old ladies.'

'You're wearing them because I said you're wearing them,' she told me. And that was that. I knew the bullies would love that and as soon as I got to school, there was a chorus of chants.

'Who do you think you are?'

'Look at Lady Muck here!'

'Think you're better than us with your posh tights, do you?'

I didn't; I didn't think that at all.

I always felt different. Not just because of Mum not caring and the abuse that had happened, but because I had been forced to grow up so quickly. I wanted to be incognito, because if they saw me, people might also see how broken and vulnerable I was. I tried to keep them at a distance and not let them get close – it did take a lot to speak out when I saw bullying but I couldn't just stand by and let it happen. I knew how hard it was to go through that sort of thing, to be attacked with no one to help. I felt like I had a mark on me, that people could see what I was if they noticed me. They would see that I was damaged and dirty, and they would know that I was a victim they could abuse if they wanted. I had some friends, the children of women Mum was friends with, and for a while I had Sally from a few doors down. I knew people, but I wasn't really close with them.

Mum was writing to Terry and visited him the whole time he was in prison and then in the hostel he was eventually released to. Mum took us to visit him at the hostel after he was released and it was then that I heard them talking about it: a mention of a 'priest', but the records I could find just say 'a homosexual'. I didn't really have a sense he had gone at all – no one told me he had killed a man, so I didn't feel it was over. I knew he would be back.

Mum wanted to fix everybody and because Terry had come from a care background, she was very much on his side and full of understanding as to why he did things, even something like killing someone. Nothing would be his fault in her mind. Normal people would think he'd been in a horrific psychotic frenzy, but she thought everything he did was understandable. I was also an incredible broken person she could have looked after – she didn't want to fix me, though.

11

'HELLO, PRINCESS'

When Terry came back to ours in 1982, I was nine. He was released from the hostel and allowed to live with us again as that was where he was registered. Everyone knew what he was and yet he was allowed back, officially released to a house with two little kids in it. It must have been a weekday as I remember coming in from school one day, soaking wet from the rain and with a gale howling about my ears. Home wasn't great, but at least it was dry.

Just before I turned the door handle, it opened and there stood Terry.

'Hello, Princess,' he smirked.

It only took one look at his face for me to feel my world had collapsed. I turned on my heels and fled, into the downpour, into the wind – anything to get away from him. I started running, but the pain in my chest wasn't from that or the cold: it was fear.

He was back.

All I could think was, *here we go again*. The primal terror consumed me and I ran and ran and ran until I couldn't run any more. Collapsing on the football field in the park, I sobbed my heart out. There was no one else there, the bleak afternoon turned into bleak early evening as my heart broke with the thought that the monster had returned.

'Come on, Della,' came a voice close to my ear as I crouched there, my head resting on my arms. 'Time to stop being so stupid. Time to come home.'

Him.

My mum couldn't even be bothered to come for me.

'I'm not coming back,' I told him.

'Why not? What's wrong with you?' he asked as if I was just being silly.

'Because of you!' I screamed. 'Because of what you do to me!' There was a thunderstorm with lightning striking all around me but Mum sent *him* out to me, rather than coming herself.

'Come on, what's up with you?' Terry shouted across the noise of the thunder.

'I've told you, I'm not going in while you're in

there.' I was determined.

'Don't be silly, I'm back now. Don't you want me back?'

'No, I don't want you to do what you were doing before. I don't want you here, Terry.'

'What do you mean, Della?' he asked, as if it wasn't obvious.

'The things! The touching, the other stuff. I don't want it. You stop, do you hear me? You stop doing it!'

'Really? You want me to stop?' he asked, as if this was a totally bewildering request.

'Yes! Yes!' The tears were running down my face, mixing with the rain, and I fully expected him to attack me there and then.

Terry stared at me as if I was something from outer space. 'OK,' he said. With that, he dragged me up by the arms and pushed me towards home. I couldn't believe his reaction. I didn't believe for a second that he meant it, I didn't believe he would ever stop.

But he did: he never touched me again.

I've had to reckon with that. If it was that easy, why didn't I ask before? Why didn't I say it in the first place? I know that the truth is that he backed off because I had voiced it and was likely to voice it to others if he kept doing it, so he could just move onto the next person, but it still sits with me.

Was it really as easy as that? Did I just have to ask?

But was that really the end of his abuse of me? No, not by a long shot, because even though he stopped touching me, he stopped making me do things, he was in my head continuously. He was abusing me mentally every second of every day. The questioning began as soon as I realised he had stopped the sexual abuse. He didn't touch me that night or the next, he didn't touch me that week or the next; he didn't touch me at all. Which made me ask myself, if all I had to do was ask, and I *hadn't* asked, then it must have been my fault that he had kept doing it.

How clever were you, Terry? How clever were you to finally get me to believe it was all down to me after all?

A few weeks after Terry came back from prison, Mum's house was broken into and I remember saying to myself, *it's alright, everyone goes through this, being raped, being abused, being robbed. You just have to get through it.* I didn't realise life didn't work like that. It was one of the ways I coped – everyone went through it. Why did I think that? What messages had I been given?

Terry did sometimes leave the house on his own now. I guess the lack of abusing me had freed up some of his time. One night, he was meant to be babysitting and Mum had already arranged to go out.

'I've got to go out now,' he said out of nowhere.

'So?' snarked Mum.

'Well, it means Della will be here on her own.'

'As I said – so? You'll have to make arrangements,' she said.

He got one of his friends to come round and sit with me. *Is he going to be the same?* I wondered. *Am I going to have to do those things with him?* I was wary but that man kept his hands off me. When it was about 10pm, this bloke said, 'I just need to nip to the shop.' He never came back.

In the morning, Mum was shouting, 'What the bloody hell happened last night? Terry, what happened?' She had come back to no one watching me and didn't think it was any of her responsibility at all, it was all Terry's fault. Apparently this man had actually gone to rob a shop and got caught breaking in when he should have been babysitting. Maybe he thought it was an alibi and he could have come back to us if he hadn't been caught in the act. Mum had a nerve given that she was out of the house every chance she got since I'd been a baby.

When Terry did go out, I had a huge sense of relief but it was even more of a relief when I was with Mum, which was why I always wanted to be by her side. I had stopped chasing after her when she went out for a while, but it had returned when Terry came back. I did expect him to start at me again. If she'd thought about why I wanted her so much, maybe things would have changed – surely they would have? I felt I could breathe if she was there, even if she was a crap mother. She never once came back when I ran after her, she'd threaten me with, 'Just you wait …' She didn't hit me as such, as I could run really fast, but she would twist her finger in my hair and turn it round so that I couldn't move, my face in hers, telling me I was bad.

Terry was still there, all the time, and there were conversations I overheard about him attacking young girls, daughters of friends, and I was just waiting for it to be me again. He had taken so much from me. I never danced in the living room or Mum's room anymore, I stayed out as much as I could. I wanted no attention on me at all. Mum's past comments about me being a drama queen or being trouble were few and far between as I was the invisible girl now. She was happy enough when I stopped hanging around her, when I realised there was no point. She could go off, looking for men, sleeping with whoever she wanted to, still on the game as far as I knew, without me hanging onto her coat. I just wanted to disappear.

I could never understand the dynamic between Mum and Terry. Yes, she did want to save people – as long as they weren't her kids – but she must have actively gone out of her way to be registered as the place Terry went back to when he was released. There was nothing sexual between them, in fact she was with his friend for a while, but even if there wasn't that element to their relationship, he had just come out of prison for a brutal killing. It was a 'frenzied attack' and that seemed to cause her no concern. She knew he was a killer, she knew he was a prolific sexual offender, and yet she still chose to bring him into her home.

I feel so angry at the social workers. On 19 April 1982, there was a report made which said: 'Terence Price was released from prison on 13 April and went to live with Carol Wright. (The Parole Officer) just found out that he was in prison with three years sentence for manslaughter – stabbed a homosexual 47 times. Also had previous convictions for indecent assault against a 12-year-old girl [. . .] Apparently, whilst in care, interfered with young girls in children's home. (Parole Officer) wanted to know our reaction to this man living with Carol Wright and I said we would be most concerned. (Parole Officer) intends to immediately get the Home Office to vary the conditions of the Parole Order so Mr Price will have to live in a probation hostel. He anticipated Mr Price would be in a hostel by tomorrow. It is also his intention to make Carol Wright aware of Mr Price's background. He will re-refer if she appears interested and he feels there is any danger of her children being exposed to abuse.'

They had known he was a repeat offender since 1980, but dismissed it all. The school told them that

I was walking the streets rather than going home and their follow-up was that they had put notes through the door. They had the opportunity then, right then, to stop the abuse almost as soon as it started. I could have been saved.

I could have been saved.

I still carry this with me, it's there as the adult I've become has grown, and the thought that someone believed popping a note through a door was enough effort compared to the effort of carrying what I do is appalling. I was never as safe as when I was in care. If they had continued with that, if they had taken me away from my mother, it would have been hard to have found something that was as bad. Instead, it was allowed into my home and into my life forever.

12

NEEDS

It was March 1982 before Mum and Dad were divorced after nine years of marriage. Dad ended up marrying Debbie, the Avon lady, and that made me feel as if he had another life. It wasn't that he didn't want anything to do with us, it was just that the split between him and Mum could never be fixed now. On the odd occasion, he would take us to their house and it was great. Debbie was lovely, a real mumsy person who always made the day special. The house was full of cats but she kept it clean and cooked delicious food. Dad would pick us up and take us there on the bus and I would be so excited to see her. But, first of all, I had to listen to all his questions about Mum:

Who's she been seeing?

Who's she been bringing round?

Has she been out all night?

Has she got a black man yet?

I'd just give quick answers – I didn't want any of

this, but I did love Dad and knew that, once I got to the house, it would be a nice day. First of all, we had to stop off at a pub where he would go in for a pint, leaving us two kids sat outside with a bottle of pop and a packet of crisps. In his own good time, we'd get to Debbie's, play on our bikes that were kept there, play with other kids and get an amazing dinner. As the visit drew to an end, she'd cuddle up with me on the sofa watching *Some Mothers Do 'Ave 'Em,* feeding me a massive knickerbocker glory and spoiling me as much as she could in the space of one day.

It would be a different world once I got back to Mum. There were all the questions from her, similar to the interrogation from Dad on the way there, but hers were always much more bitter and I felt as if I'd betrayed her by having such a nice time with Debbie. She tried to poison me against her and was always threatening to 'do something' to herself to cope with the fact that there was another woman around. In the end, it was easier to just pull away from that little bit of sunshine in my life and let Mum win. The pain of coming back was much worse than the joy I got being there; it just wasn't worth the questioning and anger.

It all came to a head one time when we got home and there was no response from Mum. Dad used to drop us at the door and hotfoot it to avoid her, and she would usually start questioning me as soon as I got in. That evening, the house was silent.

'Mum?' I shouted, shrugging my coat off and getting my little brother sorted. 'You here?' She might have gone out, leaving the door unlocked as we always got back around the same time. Something niggled me though. The telly was off – she would surely have left it on to make people think there was someone in – and it just seemed too quiet. Still calling, 'Mum? Mum?' I went through each room of the house, ending up in the bathroom. Ending up looking at my mum lying on the floor, unconscious, with blood everywhere.

'What's happened to Mum?' squealed my brother behind me. 'What's all that blood?'

'It's not blood, silly!' I told him. 'It's hair dye.'

'Why is Mum asleep then?' he asked.

'I guess it must have been taking a long time and she got tired,' I answered, unable to drag my eyes away from her. 'Come on now, let's get you to bed.' I shoved him into his room with instructions to wash his face and brush his teeth. I knew that someone had to help with this, it was too much for me, so I slipped out to our neighbour's house.

Knowing she was a nurse, I banged on her door,

begging her to help. All I know is that Mum did get taken to hospital but the guilt of what I had done weighed so heavy that I never went back to Debbie's. I stayed with Nan for a few days. She was a woman who didn't mind giving her opinion about anyone, at any time, and she had little time for Mum.

'I'm not impressed, not impressed at all, Della,' she tutted. 'She's bone idle at the best of times and now this? No, I'm not impressed at all.'

After that, Dad was always of the mind that I knew where he was if I needed him – but I wanted him to be there, I wanted someone to be there for me, not put the responsibility on me to have to seek him out. He could never commit to anything, really. Debbie and Dad stayed together for ten years but she eventually ended it as he would disappear for days, weeks, on end and the worry was too much for her. She said he never raised a hand to her, despite everything Mum had claimed about him. He threw away a lovely woman there and I wish she had been in my life much more. I loved my dad but he was selfish through and through.

*** *

The social workers were still writing files on us and they say that Mum was constantly worried that she had rent arrears and couldn't pay utility bills. From what I know and what I saw that was a deliberate ploy, trying to manipulate them, as she did have money. She would go down to the Social Services as she knew they could put her in touch with charities. I remember one in Handsworth, where we had to go upstairs into a big warehouse and she could choose what she needed. I thought that was great and once got a pair of moon boots. She hated that sort of set-up though as she wanted money, always money, not things.

The social workers came to the house sometimes to say that Mum was entitled to cash handouts and she'd dance around the room when they left. They were more concerned about that than whether I was safe – and they were so ignorant about the fact that she did have money.

The only other time I ever saw Mum happy was when she was with friends once Terry was in prison or the hostel, sometimes taking me with her or, more often, leaving me at home. I'd get a phone call from one of the other women saying I needed to meet her at the bottom of the hill and push her up as she was too drunk to walk. I was this tiny little thing going out in the dark to find her falling over, a mess, and I would either have to try and drag her up the hill or shove her from behind. She was happy enough with music, money, men and drinking, I guess. All she spoke about was men and how sexy she was – her life revolved around being wanted or needed, getting some man's attention, *any* man. She was also always sexualising me through constantly talking about sex. That's how I remember her – high on medication or drunk or in bed with a man or going out to find a man. She was completely disinterested in being a mum unless she was talking to me about sex, as if I was her best mate rather than her little girl.

Terry was only back with us for a few weeks, but moving out didn't make that much difference as he was still around. As Mum was in a relationship with one of his friends, that gave them a reason to see each other and we would also go to visit Terry in his bedsit. I had a constant fear that he could start the abuse again at any time. Appallingly, Terry had found a girlfriend very soon after he had been released and she was pregnant. It seems unbelievable to me that this was allowed – had no one spoken to her? Maybe she was fine with him being a convicted killer, but did she also dismiss the fact that he was a paedophile, or was she never told? They soon moved out to a council-provided maisonette, which showed that he must have been supported in getting that accommodation and there must have been awareness that he was going to be a father.

Seeing his pregnant girlfriend made something click in my mind – I knew that baby could be in danger from Terry, I knew it was wrong what had happened.

It would be terrifying to be born into his family and I couldn't understand why it was happening. I still didn't have the words, the language, for what Terry had done to me, but I wasn't sleeping, I was scared all the time and I felt it was a complete betrayal by my mum that I was still being forced into a world that had Terry in it. He acted very normally, as if nothing had ever happened. He was involved in his relationship and excited about the baby coming, and that worried me – I was petrified that he was excited for reasons I didn't want to think about.

The visits all took the same form, chatting, drinking, all day and into the night. It was a small bedsit with a sofa bed in the living room, a tiny kitchen area, a loo and one bedroom. There was always music blaring from the radio and a heavy fog of smoke hung around every inch of the place. I would be plonked in front of the telly, usually bribed with a video that Mum had got me earlier from the shop, which I would watch over and over again.

For some reason, Mum liked being there and there was one night when it got later and later until she decided we'd stay over. Terry and his girlfriend went to their room as I lay on the sofa bed with Mum. Terry's friend was hanging around, pouring himself a drink, and then, all of a sudden, he was there, on top of Mum.

I could hear Mum saying, 'I can't – she's awake.'

'Nah, she's fast asleep,' said Terry's friend.

'Well, she might wake up.'

'I'll be quick – she won't hear a thing, she won't notice, stop worrying,' he told her.

As Mum lay there, having sex next to me, I concentrated on listening to George Michael on the radio and doing my two times table in my head. I still do that as a way of dissociating, a way of coping. Of course, I thought that he might start on me. I froze and pretended to be asleep, but the relief of him leaving once he was done was overwhelming. To be in a position like that as a child, to have to pretend you have no idea your mum is having sex with a strange man inches away from you, marks you forever. Their bodies touched the side of me, my own body moved about on the sofa as they grunted together. It was sickening.

The next morning, Mum acted as if everything was perfectly normal.

I suppose it was.

* * *

As I've said, I always felt marked, as if my forehead had been branded and any man could see that I was damaged goods but I was still desperate for attention. The slightest act of kindness or any compliment would make me think that the person giving it was wonderful and that they would be my saviour – as long as I behaved the way they wanted. When one of my teachers – Mr Parker – started to tell me nice things, I was over the moon.

'You're a very pretty little girl, Della,' he would say.

'You have such a nice smile.'

'You always brighten up my day.'

'Look at that face – lovely!'

It was constant. Every time he passed, he would stop me and say something nice. I revelled in it. Imagine a teacher thinking I mattered? When he asked me to come to his room during break or stay after school, I thought nothing of it.

'I'd love to take some pictures of you,' he told me. 'Make sure I have a photo of that smiling face even when you aren't here!' And I did. I went to his room – while no one said a word about it. When I think I was 'lucky' that he never asked me to take my clothes off, I know that's wrong. No one should feel they are lucky that they weren't abused (again), but I have photos from those days and they remind me of all the poses he wanted me to strike. Hair thrown over my shoulder. Arms behind my head. Side-on with the look I knew he liked. Telling me I was photogenic and I'd make an amazing model. He even used to send me postcards when he went on holiday. The meetings stopped very abruptly, so perhaps someone did find out, or maybe he found a little girl who he liked better. When he stopped, I had a sense of disappointment: he'd made me feel special and now all that had ended.

There is no doubt in my mind now that he was grooming me, that he *did* groom me. Even the fact that he gave me copies makes me think that he wanted it to seem as if he was including me, that I was willing, if anything did come of it.

13

NO ESCAPE

There was no sex education until I was in the first year of senior school. We were shown a film of people in a swimming pool, all naked, and the main characters were an old man and a young girl – which reinforced to me that my experiences with Terry had been the norm. The voiceover spoke about bodies and what happened in puberty, but the age gap between the two main characters made me feel that there hadn't been anything wrong with what had gone on. I still didn't have the words for what had happened by watching it and it was all about reproductive systems rather than sexual acts.

For some reason, around the time I was in first year, Mum decided to start writing to an old boyfriend she had known when she was in care. Harry lived in Wales, which meant that she began dragging me there to see him. Eventually, she declared it was true love and we were going to move to Colwyn Bay to be with him. She let her sister, Anna, move into the house – covering herself if things didn't work out with Harry, as she'd still have the tenancy – and life was turned upside down. It turned out to be one of the best experiences I ever had. I loved it there and Harry was an incredibly nice man. His whole family was lovely, even his parents used to take me on days out.

The house we moved into was an old Victorian property with big windows and huge rooms. Upstairs were flats he had converted. There was a girl from Liverpool in one of them, Gillian, and she became a good friend for the few months I lived there. While I was there, the sea and the parks and the house were all like a dream come true. It was at the high school with Gillian that I got a feel for what a normal life was like. I'd never had that before and it was wonderful. My life had a breath of fresh air – no one knew me, which meant that I could be myself. Mum was working in an old people's home and every night Harry would make us a big family dinner, giving me the chance to pretend this was my life now.

It only lasted a few months and then we went back to Birmingham. I was absolutely gutted – that time was the highlight of my childhood. It was the longest time

I had ever been with a man who was completely good, but Mum messed it up as usual. Even with Harry's dad, who took me out for the day quite often, I didn't have to try and be on his good side to keep myself safe – he just liked me for who I was and enjoyed spending time with me. There was no bad side to them.

When we got back to Birmingham, I found out someone I knew, Gail, had reported to the police that her partner had abused her daughter, Rosie, who I was friends with. The police came to our house and questioned me because I was friends with Rosie. The way they framed the questions was appalling and made me realise what I would have faced if I'd ever reported anyone. They said that she was flirty, that she had probably led him on. I knew I wouldn't say anything if that was how they dealt with it. They dropped the case as it was just Rosie's word against his. That moment, when the police showed me how they were, was a moment I'll never forget. It's as if there was a path and if they had dealt with it in a different way, maybe I would have disclosed what had happened to me with the family friend or even Terry. They effectively closed ranks, suggesting she was causing trouble because she didn't like him and that if anything had happened, she wanted it.

I was 12 at that point. I'd had the lovely time in Wales but it was back to reality now, a reality where children were not believed, where even the good guys had a narrative of dirty little girls leading men on. All of these messages were coming together: there was no point in speaking out, as I knew I wouldn't be believed and I'd just be cast as a little slut. Why would I make trouble for myself?

It had been about a year since Terry had been released and the further away the abuse was, the more I thought that people would be even less likely to believe me – why hadn't I spoken out then? Why had I left it so long? When Rosie made her report, it cemented in my mind that what Terry had done was really wrong and that was the first time that I truly understood how bad it had been. Reminders of the abuse were everywhere. I'd go to the precinct in Newtown with friends and there was a flasher who wore Michael Jackson's 'Thriller' outfit. He'd stand there all day exposing himself and girls were just meant to laugh it off, minimise what he was doing. But men flashing aren't going to stop at that, are they? There must be so many of them who progress to other things, but women are just meant to accept it. Men could do what they wanted – not even just sexually – they could do what they wanted full stop. When I looked at what Nan had let her sons get away with, it was staggering. Robbing, owning guns, police raids on the house, bringing all the stolen stuff back – it was all fine, as they were her boys and that was the culture women just had to accept.

By the time we got back from Wales, Terry was out of our lives. He seemed to just disappear and I was never taken to see him again. Mum had a new boyfriend, a Nigerian man, and she was so delighted that she finally had a black man that she didn't bother with Terry or anyone associated with him. Aaron thought he was better than everyone. He would tell them that he was a prince, from a hugely respected, rich family, which gave him airs and graces. Mum acted just as superior as him. He was a lot younger than her and she loved it, telling anyone who would listen that he was obsessed with her. Everyone knew that he was just after a visa, apart from Mum, who was wilfully blind to that side of their relationship.

Aaron had moved in within weeks of them meeting and their wedding happened in a flash too in 1986. It was a registry office do, with a big party afterwards. My Uncle Neville, who was adopted, had an Asian girlfriend – Auntie Jojo – who got on with Mum and her new partner. The wedding party was at their house, with loads of people there. I did like my Uncle Neville he was all spliffs and music and seemed different to the other men in our family – but I hated that they were friends with Mum. She was the centre of attention that night, which was all she ever wanted, to be the belle of the ball. There were loads of Aaron's Nigerian friends there too, which made her ooze confidence, thinking they all fancied her and that Aaron was a lucky man.

She was a bit nicer to me at this point, I suppose, but Aaron was horrible. He started laying down laws very quickly, deciding that I had done something wrong out of nowhere. He believed that women needed to do as they were told, that I should be doing lots of chores, be in at a certain time, do everything he said. I did rebel against it – who was this man telling me what to do? I wanted to be out of the house as often as possible. I argued with Mum about who the hell he thought he was, but she was blinded by lust. She spent all her money on him too. At one point, I really wanted a new style for my bedroom, with a patterned quilt cover, some fancy silky curtains and whatnot. Mum, in a rare good mood, promised that I could have it. But then Aaron decided that I had done something wrong, I can't even remember what it was, and she spent the money on him instead. That brought back memories of Terry for me, saying that I would get the Elvis doll. Mum was very generous with other people, throwing her money around on them, but still telling the social workers that she had nothing.

By now, Nan had moved just round the corner from us and I spent as much time there as possible. Uncle Tommy still lived at home, he was only five years older than me, and I started hanging out with him and his friends. One of his friends was called Jason.

And he was the start of the next horrific phase of my life.

* * *

I was drawn to being with older kids, not that they were kids, really. They let me smoke and I felt more grown-up around them. At least I wasn't being ignored as I was at home; I had somewhere to escape to.

I was only about 13 or 14 when I started going out with Jason.

I was out of the house so much with my Uncle Tommy and his friends, including Jason. He was nice at first, we'd have fun and be out all day at Sutton Park, swimming in the lakes, coming home on the bus, filthy dirty but having had great laughs as we were out and free. But it didn't last: I always felt that people could see something in me, they could see I was worthless. Sometimes my Uncle Tommy would come round and babysit for us, when I was 11 or 12. When Tommy came, he brought Jason and it didn't feel like there was much of an age difference. We'd all dance around the living room to MTV, but the process was starting all over again. One thing that sticks in my mind is this flowered headband which Jason used to get me to wear when I was dancing and he'd always say how grown-up I looked in it. I'd dance about and it was another grooming process starting again, me getting attention and him knowing exactly what he was doing. He liked me to do my hair in a certain way, too.

He was around with Tommy for a while and then when I was about 12 or 13, he kissed me for the first time. Frankie Goes to Hollywood, 'The Power of Love' was out and I remember that playing. It was at a New Year's Eve party. Jason was nice to me at that point.

'I've always liked you, Della, you're so pretty,' he told me and I lapped it up.

It felt right. He had been there for so long and it felt natural. At first, the physical abuse was a joke. He and Tommy would do legs and wings (where each person holds a leg and arm and they swing you around), but they would chuck me at a wall. It would end with me having bruises all up my legs and back. We'd go swimming and I would be covered in marks. Even my uncle thought it was funny, whereas I now think Jason was seeing where my boundaries were. I had none – they'd all been smashed.

He had two sisters and we used to babysit their kids – that's where a lot of the sex happened, when the kids were in bed. I was 13 and he was nearly 19.

The first time it happened was at Nan's house. Her next-door neighbour had strangled his wife as he was having an affair with a neighbour and wanted to start a new life with her. He killed her and hid her body in his outside shed. The police did all the forensics and boarded up the house once they worked out what had happened, but for my uncles, that was just another opportunity. They had no morals, so they went and robbed the house. They stole the bed that poor woman was murdered in – as well as loads more stuff – and brought it back to Nan. It was next door so Uncle Tommy would only have had to put it over the small fence that divided the gardens. My nan would have known and may have even helped him. You have to remember that those boys could do nothing wrong in her eyes, including keeping the bed of a dead woman in the house, the bed she was actually strangled in.

The first time I had sex was on that bed.

I was more terrified because I knew the history of the bed than about what Jason was doing to me. I was thinking, *he wants this and women don't have a say, so best just get it over and done with. You say that and you talk about it with your friends, and they are all saying the same thing.* I did wonder if I would bleed the first time because I thought of it as my first time. I had to really, the truth was so horrific. I wondered about what pain I would go through, while blocking out what had already happened to me. I have this vivid recollection of lots of coins in the back pocket of my jeans. When he'd finished, I got up off the bed and thought, *God, there's blood everywhere! On a dead woman's bed!* It was just the shape of the coins in the dark though, as they'd fallen out everywhere. Was there part of me that thought I was a virgin? I read something recently which made sense. Often medical forms will ask when you first became sexually active, but for someone with my history, what do you put? Was it when I was 13, or was it when I was just a little girl?

Jason wasn't someone you wanted to get on the wrong side of. He had a horrible temper, but I felt grown-up: I was in a relationship. Tommy was with his girlfriend, Brenda, and I wanted to be in this close little gang, a foursome of two couples madly in love. They were all about 19 though and I was still so very young. The sex continued whenever Jason wanted and whenever there was an opportunity.

It didn't take long for the violence to start. He battered me, I was covered in bruises from head to toe and no one ever questioned where those bruises came from. We'd be at his sister's and he would kick off for no reason and have no hesitation in hitting me in front of one of them. One time, we were on our way through a park and he started slapping me outside her maisonette as she looked out to see if we were on our way. He said that I made him angry, that I was stupid, but it was all made up. Anything I did would have been wrong. I never knew if I would get Nasty Jason or Nice Jason, but given that I needed to get an injunction against him eventually, Nasty Jason was much more in evidence.

14

THIS IS YOUR LIFE

Jason and I had been together for about a year when I realised that I was pregnant. I started feeling sick in the morning and realised I'd missed a period. There used to be pregnancy clinics you could just pop into, with a urine sample and no need for an appointment. I must have picked up knowing about that from the older girls as Brenda was pregnant by then. When they told me the result was positive, I just thought I would be in the shit with Mum. She was actually fine about it, which was weird – why wasn't she bothered? But she was very laid-back and I thought that was me with Jason forever now, that was my future. I was stuck. By this time, he was cheating on me too and that was all laid out in front of me as my life.

At that time, I had a friend called Kelly who lived near Nan; they were from an Irish family and her home was a lovely place to be. Her parents, Jill and Nick, were such kind people. Jill loved her bingo, like Nan, and she always liked Kelly to be in to do her hair before she went. It was such a little thing, but I wished I had a life like that. Kelly became my best friend and I spent more time at Nan's and hers than I did at home. It was a completely different environment – they had rules but they were really good parents, a complete contrast to my house.

I had to move schools as the senior school I went back to in Birmingham hadn't worked out as I was bullied so badly. I went to Kelly's school which was Catholic, even though I wasn't. It was much nicer there. I'd go to her house every morning and always had to wait for her as she washed and blow-dried her beautiful bobbed hair every single day. One day, I wasn't feeling great as soon as I got there but by the time we were on the bus, the most awful cramps were flooding my body. Kelly grabbed my arm and got me home. I was clinging to her as I almost fell in the door and she manoeuvred me onto the sofa.

'Oh God, I'm bleeding!' I screamed.

I was only about eight weeks pregnant and the pain shouldn't have been like that, even if I was miscarrying. It was excruciating. Mum called an ambulance and

I was taken to hospital, where no one really spoke to me. They all spoke over me, to Mum, and it was terrifying. It was an ectopic pregnancy, but at least my fallopian tubes hadn't burst as that would have been life-threatening. No one was questioning why a 14-year-old was pregnant and no one explained what was involved to me. They told Mum that I might need my fallopian tubes removed and could be in a position where I would never be able to have kids. I was hearing it all going on, thinking, *what the hell?* No one thought that I should be spoken to directly. When I was under anaesthetic, they also found cysts on my ovaries, which were removed through the laparoscopy (which was keyhole surgery into my abdomen), and also gave me a D&C (dilation and curettage) to remove whatever tissue was left of my baby. No one explained how much pain there would be after that. The next day I was sent home and I literally could not walk.

I was 14. I'd just heard that I might never have kids and was simply left to it. Again, my body wasn't my own, other people had decided what was going to happen to it. Mum got to sign all the forms as I was a minor and everyone else just spoke about me as if I wasn't there.

What were the repercussions on me psychologically? I'm not sure I've ever processed it, I'm not sure you ever do. I have realised how much I dissociate now.

Some people have different versions of themselves to take over and cope with various situations or triggers – I have a legion of different emotional Dellas. Some shut off, others take charge depending on what I need to face or get through. You become a shadow and as a protective measure, you shut down certain emotions to deal with things and protect yourself.

Losing a baby was just another thing that happened to me. Mum took me to the doctors to get the depo injection as that was an easy option for her, a decision made between her and the GP: get me jabbed for three months worth of contraception and forget about it. There were no questions about me being sexually active and I was never taken back for the second injection. Mum never questioned why I was with a man so much older than me and she never really questioned how Jason acted with me. He wasn't comforting or there for me in any way when I lost the baby and he soon ramped up how nasty he was.

In the kitchen one day, he had me by the throat, rammed up against the wall. I managed to get out of his grip and ran upstairs. There was a big commotion with me screaming, 'Get him off me!'

Mum was there that day and she came flying up to me.

'What do you think you're doing?' she shouted at Jason. 'Get off her!'

I was sobbing my heart out and as he was yelling at me, he said, 'You're absolutely disgusting, do you know that? Not like your mum – she's fit, I'd do her.'

In that moment, Mum changed. I was being battered, he'd tried to strangle me, but she was preening on the staircase because my boyfriend had said he'd have sex with her. I was distraught and she had just witnessed the violence, but she was never happier than when men wanted her. Even though she was with Aaron and that was apparently all she had ever wanted, she never stopped looking for affirmation from men.

There was no follow-up care for the ectopic pregnancy and my life went back to 'normal', back to the relationship with Jason. I went back to my Catholic school quite quickly, even though I wasn't really ready for it. Even at that young age, 14, you start planning in your head. I had wanted that baby. All I could imagine was someone I could love and who could love me, someone who could make my life better, and that had been snatched away from me.

Sitting in class that first day back, suddenly it all hit me and I began to cry.

'I'm not having this,' my teacher said. 'If there's something bothering you, go and see one of the pastoral care team rather than upsetting my class.'

All of the student advisors were priests. As I stumbled from the classroom to see the one allocated to my year group, I made a decision: I was going to tell someone. I was going to tell this priest what had been done to me by Terry, how I felt and why the tears just wouldn't stop falling.

I had barely sat down when it all came out. Every word of it came from my heart as if a dam had been opened and the flood couldn't be stopped. The priest sat behind his desk while I broke down. Finally, I paused for breath and he sighed.

'Why are you saying these things, Della?' he asked. 'You should not – ever – be talking to me or anyone else in this way. These are nasty, disgusting words coming from your mouth. This is not the time or the place, and you must think about your actions. These are wicked things, wicked words. You need to leave and never mention this again.'

All I could think was, *I can't talk to anybody, this is all my fault.* He was an adult and he was also a priest. Surely, he could help? Surely, he would have a moral obligation to do something for me? I went back to class, still in floods of tears. The teacher never mentioned it at all. Kelly was always kind, but I never told her about the abuse, which meant she just thought it was about the baby.

I didn't want to be with Jason anymore. I did everything I could to avoid him: I would go to different places, not be where he would think I might be. But he was having none of it and it got to a stage where I couldn't even leave the house. He was always outside, always watching and waiting to say nasty things as soon as I set foot outside. Eventually, the one thing Mum ever did for me was take an injunction out on him so that he wasn't meant to come anywhere near me. It didn't stop him though and it got to the point where I was terrified to leave the house on my own. My nan's brother was with someone who had a son from a previous relationship, called Robert. He stepped up to be a sort of protector, my knight in shining armour.

'Anywhere you need to go, Della, just let me know and I'll make sure that bastard doesn't get near you, OK?' Robert was 19, working, and he made me feel like I was being looked after. For about six months, we hung out together. He really was watching out for me, paying for everything, even taking me to clubs, which gave me a bit of normality, I thought – although there shouldn't have been anything normal about a 14-year-old hanging out with a grown man who was nearly 20. I soon found myself in a relationship with Robert.

After I'd lost the baby, Aaron, my stepdad, did change. From someone who had been really controlling about what a woman or girl's place was in the house, he became very kind. Mum was working in a children's home at the top of our road (trying to save anyone but me, as usual) and Aaron would make me nice meals, chat to me, tell me about the music he liked. Suddenly, he was the grown-up in our house and he would tell me I was intelligent and how much he enjoyed our conversations. He framed things differently now, not telling me to do things round the house like I was a slave any longer but asking if I could 'help out' with housework, tidying, doing the dishes. He treated me like an equal and looking back, I feel so stupid.

One night I went to bed and he came into my room to say goodnight as he always did when Mum was at work. He looked at me with a gaze I never wanted to see and told me, 'I just really want to kiss you, Della.' His arm went round the back of me as he loomed closer and my mind went straight to, *not again – I'm not doing this again.* I froze for a moment before telling him no – no, no, no! Aaron did go to his own room but there was a lingering fear in me: was it starting over? The next day, I told Robert, who was very supportive and said that I needed to tell Mum. This wasn't long after she had been sat watching a programme about abuse.

She'd said, 'If that had happened to one of mine, I would kill whoever did it.'

That made me feel like she might actually take me seriously. I was pregnant again, with Robert's baby, having just found out. I didn't want to bring a child into this. It was dangerous – I needed to speak to her about what Aaron was doing.

'I need to talk to you about something,' I told her.

'Spit it out then.'

'No, not here – I'll meet you at Nan's house this afternoon.'

'Ever the drama queen – just tell me, can't you?'

But I stood my ground: I couldn't do it in that house, not where Aaron lived.

Nan was really supportive when I told her what was going on. I guess that was because no one was asking her to do anything and she wasn't having to defend 'her boys'.

'That's a bloody disgrace,' she exploded. 'I knew he was a bad 'un – we all did. Typical of your bloody mother to get shackled to a waste of time like that. She has to know, Della, she has to kick him out.'

When Mum came in, I told her what Aaron had done: 'I'm not comfortable being in the house while you're working nights. He's making me feel it's not right. I just need to tell you that he's tried to kiss me.'

She was shocked but around the same time, her friends had been telling her that he had been coming on to them and that he wasn't trustworthy. She had dismissed all of that, said they were jealous that she had this amazing man. I knew as I'd be there sometimes, when they were talking and telling her that he was slimy, he was making advances to them, he wasn't to be trusted. I knew her response to them so I thought she wasn't going to believe me as I had already heard the responses to her friends. I was really surprised by her reaction, maybe because Robert and Nan were there.

'I am so, so sorry,' she wept. 'I didn't realise any of this was going on. I'm going to go home now, tell him to pack his bags and get out.'

I was incredibly relieved. I hadn't expected it to go the way it had. Maybe this time she would be there for me.

15

A LIGHT IN THE DARKNESS

The night I told Mum about my stepfather, I did have some hope. Maybe I could tell her about Terry. I didn't really dream of doing it back when I was a child, I didn't feel I could tell her and she would fix it, but this could be a new beginning.

She did get Aaron to leave and I felt like I could breathe again: I was actually being believed. Mum got in touch with Social Services the next day and told them what had been going on. I think because I had told her in front of people, she felt she had no choice but to be seen to be doing something about it. They asked if they could interview us separately – me and Mum first. She went in and spoke to them; they spoke to Aaron at a later date.

A report a few weeks later says:

(Social worker) is very concerned about Della Wright. Mrs Wright informed him that Della told her that her stepfather had been making advances towards her. As a result, Mrs Wright told her co-hab to get his belongings out of her house and to leave them alone. This he did two or three weeks ago. Currently Della is relatively safe as she is living alone with her mother.

Past history that may still be affecting Della:

Della was pregnant last March – her boyfriend was verbally and physically abusive towards her. As a result, she miscarried. While in hospital, they found a cyst for which she had an operation.

On her return to school, she made attempts to discuss her problems with her teachers. She was crying at the time so the teachers sent her back to her class and said that she was wasting their time. As a result, she refused to return to school.

Mrs Wright's ex-boyfriend is demanding money from her and he has threatened her.

Mother has taken injunction against Della's ex-boyfriend to prevent him entering the house. Della is receiving home teaching. Mrs Wright does not want social work intervention because she believes that we may take her daughter into care.

Della stated that her stepfather had first started to make improper advances towards her in June/July. These incidents always occurred when her mother was out of the house. When Della reported the situation to Mrs Wright she put Aaron (stepfather) out of the house.

While that might all look quite supportive on paper, the reality was that they wrote Aaron's behaviour up as 'fatherly affection' in the end. I now know why: Mum had told them that I was probably just making it up as I was upset about losing the baby and I wasn't myself. Then when Aaron spoke to them, he said he was just trying to be paternal, that I had misunderstood what he was saying. The Social Services said we needed family therapy.

'There's no way I'm going to that!' I said.

I had been building up the courage to tell Mum about Terry but now I was on the back foot again. Mum didn't outwardly say she didn't believe me but the atmosphere was different after that. I remember going out, coming back, still not knowing if I was safe. I walked upstairs to the living room and I saw Aaron standing there with nothing but a towel round him.

What the hell? I thought. *What is he doing here?*

I went absolutely mental: 'What are you doing bringing *him* back into the house?'

'We've spoken about it and you got it wrong, Della. It wasn't what you thought it was,' Mum said.

'I can't do this,' I told her.

With that, I left home at 15, pregnant. Social Services

were well aware of all this but there was no follow-up. I moved in with Robert at his dad and step mum's for a little bit. I was back at school. At first the relationship with him was OK. It wasn't great, he wasn't perfect, but it was when we got a flat together that it got bad – his parents kept him in line, I think. My school was just down the road, but as I started to get bigger and show more, I was sent to a school for pregnant schoolgirls in Erdington. Robert and his step mum didn't get on – we were there for two weeks and then they had an argument over something silly, and she told us to get out. I was now homeless as well as pregnant. What the hell were we going to do?

My uncle told us, 'I've got a flat you can come and stay at,' and we had no choice but to go there. I then had to go to the Housing Department and make a homelessness application. I'd got someone from Social Services to come with me as I didn't know what the hell I was doing. I was filling out the forms and noticed that you had to be over 16 – I wasn't that age yet. So I changed my date of birth on the form and the man was interviewing me and realised I had lied. He screamed at me in the middle of the Housing Department office.

'Do you realise you'll get prosecuted now? DO YOU?' he yelled.

I did, I guess, but I had no choice: 'What do you want me to do?'

The social worker with me spoke with him: 'You must see that these are exceptional circumstances? She's pregnant and homeless – it's not her fault that she's 15. You can see why she's done what she's done.'

Thankfully, they did give me a flat, and it was when I moved into it with Robert that he started to be abusive. If we had an argument, he would lean himself out the window of the flat, saying he was going to throw himself down on to the ground. He would put a belt round his neck and say he would hang himself – he was mentally abusive every chance he got. Before we got together, he had wanted to join the Navy and he went back to that notion.

'I'm not ready to be a dad, I'm going to join the Navy and you'll just have to bring this kid up on your own.' He threw that at me all the time. We were together for 11 years and the abuse carried on throughout. I wanted to do everything possible to know my child had a stable home, so I put up with it all. Just after we moved into that flat, we got engaged – I was 15 – and we had a party, kids playing grown-ups. My dad came and I thought he would go mad when he saw my big belly.

'It was obvious something like this was going on or you wouldn't be bloody getting engaged at 15, would you?' he said. He brought Debbie with him. I was so young, having all this adult responsibility that I didn't know what to do with. I was scared, but when I went to that school in Erdington, all the girls were in the same position. We were taught how to make baby quilts and do nice things for our babies. They treated us like humans, not mistakes.

Throughout the pregnancy, Robert wasn't supportive – I remember going to an antenatal appointment late on and something wasn't right, they couldn't feel the baby moving.

'You'll have to go to hospital, immediately.'

I went to hospital and phoned him at work at the factory, telling him something wasn't right, but he left me to it. The baby was fine, but that was how he was.

It was so triggering having Laura. One of the best and worst experiences I could have had. It was a vaginal delivery and I tore, which was awful. The midwives were amazing; one of them was helping me towards the end of her shift but she stayed with me until the end.

'I can see my partner waiting out there with our kids – they need to go to school,' she told me, 'but there's no way I'm leaving you. I'm here until the end, Della. Let's get this baby out.' I bless her to this day.

I remember looking up at the ceiling and I could see blood.

Dear God, I remember thinking, *what happens when you give birth? How in the world does blood get up there?*

Robert was there, but he wasn't much use.

'Just give her some encouragement,' the midwife said, 'she's almost there.'

But he didn't even know where to start and did nothing.

Having contractions, it hits you that there's no way back. The fear of not being in control of your body – again – is enormous. With Laura, it wasn't as bad as it would be with my later births, because I was so young and naïve, but it got worse with each one.

Laura was the light in my world from the moment she arrived. You get this overwhelming love at the same time as being petrified. It was worse because she was a girl. I was flooded with love at the same time as terror covering me. How would I do this? How would I protect her? There were so many beasts in my own family – how did I keep this precious bundle safe?

When she was born, they wanted me to give her a bath but I couldn't do it. It was too much responsibility – I had this rush of feeling, thinking, *how the hell am I going to get this baby to adulthood safely? I couldn't protect myself when I was little, how can I protect her?* I was terrified. There were all these bad people in the world, how could I keep her away from them? The midwives actually used her as a demonstration for other mums to do baths and stuff as I couldn't do it. I was terrified. It was traumatic and I now had a massive responsibility – it was scary beyond belief.

Laura was beautiful, such a good baby, but I just wanted her for me. I hated everyone wanting to hold her, I wanted her to myself. I never ever left her on her own with anyone and I hated it when Mum passed her around.

'Give her back now,' I'd say.

One of the first times I took her out, Mum completely took over. She wanted to push the pram, barging me out of the way, wanting to take over like Laura was her baby. She wanted to be the perfect nan as she knew she had been a rubbish mum. She undermined me so much, always telling me what was the right way, and I'd think, *you can talk, you weren't great at it, were you?*

Just after we brought her home, a couple of days later, my mum came round with all her friends. They were passing her to each other and I felt sick. I didn't want these people intruding, but Mum had decided, almost as if she was her baby. I couldn't settle Laura and was convinced it was because of this. To me, it was like when a puppy or other baby animal is touched by people and the smell is wrong to the mum. Everyone else had their hands on her and it didn't feel right to my maternal instinct.

16

MY BABY

I didn't have postnatal depression which, in retrospect, was surprising. About a month after I had Laura, it was Robert's 21st birthday party. We had all gone out and had a lovely time at a club. My cousin, Bernard, was living with us in the flat as he was homeless. We all got back and I went to bed with Robert, then during the night, I woke up to feel someone's hand on my leg.

I remember thinking, *what the hell is going on here?*

I was frozen; I always froze.

It was Bernard. I rolled over and put my arm over my boyfriend. He left when I did that. That should have been the safest place in the world for me, in my own home, in my own bed, sleeping next to my partner. I woke up the next morning feeling physically sick, just needing to get out of my own house. If he felt emboldened enough to do something like that when Robert was inches away, what else would he feel confident enough to do?

I had to get out of there. Mum had looked after the baby, which meant she wasn't in the flat when it happened; had she been there, that would have completely thrown me. I wouldn't go back there while my cousin was – he was constantly in and out, treating it like his own place. When I had left home at 15 and Mum was still with Aaron, she then moved in with him to his house. When I was pregnant, if I wanted to see my mum or my brother, I had to accept he was there and it was now his house. It didn't happen often, as I'd try to meet her at other places. After I had Laura, she had gone off the rails and was having problems with Aaron. She'd had a phantom pregnancy when she found out I was going to be a mum and she went missing for days on end, eventually coming back without ever really explaining things, but it was getting worse at this stage. She went to the Housing Department and was told that she could have a four-bedroom new build if she said that I needed to move in with her. Until the incident with my cousin, I would never have agreed, but that changed things: I needed to get away from him.

'I'll move in with you,' I finally agreed.

That was a huge thing. I'd been abused under her watch, she'd let me down for years, but I had a constant hope she would change. I just needed to find the right environment, the right time, then I'd get the right mum. I always held onto that. Even though she was trying to take over with Laura and telling me that I wasn't doing the right things, I always had that hope. It's not until you come out of that – and I hadn't been out for long – that you can see other options. I was still so young, not worldly-wise at all, and I wanted a family unit. I would have had to break away completely to see how messed-up things were.

Robert, Laura and I all moved in with Mum before Christmas. When I was pregnant, I'd been working in a nightclub in Birmingham, collecting glasses, but I got too big to actually bend over the tables for them. I was moved to cloakroom duties and I was still there when we moved into that house. A couple of days before Christmas 1989, we'd gone out to have a drink with Nan for her birthday before heading to work afterwards. Robert was so drunk and when he got to work, he was vomiting in the toilets with everyone lying to management about his whereabouts. I bundled him into a taxi and sent him home as he was absolutely paralytic, then stayed on to finish my shift. Mum was looking after Laura, but what I didn't know was that she had gone out and left my brother to babysit.

Finally, my shift was over at 3am and I could get back to Laura.

As I approached the house, there seemed to be a strange light coming from it. The closer I got, the faster my heart beat – it wasn't light, it was fire. There was smoke pouring from the building and all I could think was, *my baby's in there!* The Fire and Rescue Service was on strike at the time and there were Army Green Goddesses parked on the street. The door was open as I raced towards it and pushed through the smoke. It was too thick, I couldn't get up the stairs. As far as I knew, everyone was in there – Robert, my brother, Mum … and my three-month-old baby.

It turned out that Mum had gone out and left my brother in charge of Laura. He was only 14 and had decided to make himself something to eat with the chip pan. He'd fallen asleep in the living room while waiting for it to cook, but had thankfully shut the living room door and with it being a new house, all the doors were fire doors. Laura was with him and the smoke hadn't got too bad in there. Robert was so drunk that he had collapsed on the bed after I sent him home from work, but had fallen off at some point when the smoke started and that's what saved him.

When the Army brought them out, my brother had a black face, Robert was covered too, the house was wrecked. It was pandemonium.

And Laura?

She was safe in the arms of one of the soldiers. Even now, I can't help but think *what if?* There is such a primal fear to fire, it's so quick and so powerful. In that moment, my whole world crashed. Everything I had was tied up in that little baby and I was helpless. They had all been so careless of her safety. Looking at that tiny body in the arms of a soldier, with a mask bigger than her head, hit me like a brick wall. Her clothes were covered in ash, her skin covered in black, but she was alive. Someone was responsible for this.

It was chaos. They took me, Laura and Robert in one ambulance, with my brother in another one. Robert was out of it, but when he came round in the ambulance and saw Laura like that in my arms, he didn't know what to do. All I could do was cuddle her. I was in shock but when we got to the hospital, I started to get more of a sense of it all. No one knew where Mum was and I never did find out.

We were placed in cubicles next door to each other, with Laura being looked after and getting oxygen.

'Will she be OK, will she be OK?' I kept asking, over and over.

'She was lucky,' the doctor told me. '*Very* lucky – but she'll be fine.'

My brother was only a teenager and he tried to make a joke of it. Robert punched his lights out.

If it hadn't been a new house with fire doors, I would have lost my baby. I felt so guilty that I had ever left her. I had been expecting Mum to be looking after her, which meant that I couldn't really blame anyone else.

The house had to be gutted. I didn't even have baby clothes for Laura and we all had to go stay with my nan. On my guard constantly, I couldn't really ever relax or enjoy anything as I was always aware that the baby could be in danger. Laura had almost died and there was never going to be a moment I could let my guard down about the chance of anything ever happening to her again.

My relationship with Robert was very strained, we didn't really get on. I only stayed at Nan's for a couple of weeks but by the time we got back to Mum's, she knew we were arguing and enjoyed that very much.

When Laura was about two months old, Brenda – Uncle Tommy's girlfriend – asked me to go out with her.

'There's a disco on at a local pub, it'll be a laugh.'

'No, I'm not long after having a baby, it's really not for me. I don't want to go out, to be honest.'

'You're 16, you need to live!'

She persuaded me and off we went. It was actually a pub Mum used to go to as it was near where we originally lived when I was a baby. I had a good time, having a laugh with Brenda. Mum was looking after Laura, even though Robert was meant to, and she wasn't happy at all. She insisted Robert take her down to the pub and left Laura with my brother.

Robert stormed in, shouting before he was even at me. When I saw him barging his way over, I was ready for his words – but not ready to see Mum storming over behind him.

'I'm not going, Robert – I'll leave when I'm ready, which won't be long anyway.' I don't know what Mum had said to him, but he went ballistic and tried to drag me out.

'You get home now,' Mum snarled. 'Don't you dare defy me.'

'What is your problem, Carol?' asked Brenda. 'You're behind this, you're making it worse – what's it got to do with you anyway? Who's she harming?' In a flash, Mum's hand slapped Brenda across the face.

'How dare you?' I shouted. 'How dare you come here and make such a scene? I'm not going, you need to leave.'

They did, but not without all sorts of cursing and attitude, and I tried to enjoy myself with Brenda. We were just sitting on our own, chatting, not bothering anyone. Robert had gone off in a huff, but Mum kept riling him up, telling him that he didn't know what types were in that pub. 'That place is full of drug dealers and pimps,' she apparently kept saying, winding him up so much that he came back, with just my brother in tow this time.

'You shouldn't be here – you've no right to be here, not with a baby at home. You should be ashamed of yourself.'

He dragged me outside as I screamed, 'I'm not going, leave me alone! Don't be ridiculous, I'm only chatting to Brenda – what do you think's going on? I'm perfectly fine, leave me alone!'

'Shut up! You're doing what I tell you and I'm telling you it's time to get out of this dive!' He was getting really physical, trying to drag me along the road, but I was having none of it to the point where – I don't really know what happened – but I think he must have punched me. I ended up on the ground and he kicked me full-on in the face. My nose exploded and I had to go to A&E, get X-rays and tell a doctor what had happened.

I was completely honest about it: 'My boyfriend kicked me in the face.'

'Is that right?'

'Yeah, I was only out with a friend and he dragged me out before he did that.'

'Well, we'll get it sorted.'

That was all they said, they never called the police or even asked if I wanted to take it further.

So, Mum knew that we were having issues – she knew really well because so much of it was encouraged by her. I didn't understand about manipulation back then, it was just how she was. She was my mum and I was in that bubble, it was just how my family was.

I focused on providing for Laura – I wanted a job and I wanted us to be stable as a family. Even though my relationship with Robert was rocky, to say the least, I thought I could make us a real family if I just tried hard enough. I tried to find work, getting an interview in the jewellery quarter in Birmingham. That really sticks out in my mind because the man said to me, 'What are you doing, love? You're just young – you've got a little baby.'

'I want to make sure she never wants for anything, I need to work,' I told him.

'Love, you go home and look after your baby.'

I was determined though. She needed to have everything. I went to a factory that made electric blankets and got a job soldering the components. I did that for a little while but the voice of that man wouldn't leave my head. He was right, all I wanted was to be with Laura. I was so torn. I wanted to give her everything and I was the only one I could rely on for that – but I wanted to protect her too and I was the only one I could rely on for that as well. So I went back to my baby. I thought that if I could stay with her until she went to school, I could be the main influence in her life and she would know she was loved.

Mum was still trying to take over with Laura and I constantly questioned myself – could I do this or would I be like her? I was so sure I wouldn't be the same sort of mother that I'd had, but there was always that fear. She was fanning the flames between me and Robert then they ended up having a fight in the house. We had a bar in the corner of the living room with a solid onyx top and, somehow, she got pushed into it. The bar cracked and she started screaming, 'He's got to leave! He's got to leave!'

'Well, if he's leaving, I'm leaving,' I told her.

And we did.

17

THE CENTRE OF ATTENTION

We got a house for the three of us, just down by the Villa ground in Aston. It was a block of flats and we were on the 13th floor, with a view of the football ground. It was really nice on match days but I quickly became quite isolated, being up there with a baby. Laura was turning into such a happy, good little thing. I did manage to feel proud of myself that I was protecting her, there was a sense of achievement in that. I had her to myself most of the time, but as she was becoming more independent, I wanted another baby so badly. I loved having Laura and wanted to prove that I could look after her and any other children I had. There was a sense of fulfilment for me in being a mum and it gave me a place in the world. That was the first time I'd had such feelings and I wanted to do it again, to have another little one that I would adore and keep safe. I got pregnant pretty much on Laura's first birthday, when I was just 17. I'd have two little kids when I wasn't much more than a child myself.

I was still in an environment where people thought abuse was acceptable and no one ever did anything about it – I just thought that was what life was. I was stuck in a flat, in a bad relationship, but I didn't know there was a way out. I thought that if I had a tight family unit, everything would be wonderful. That was all I wanted. It was all about making sure the kids had a better life than I'd had – I was so naïve. I was in a rotten relationship but still kept those rose-tinted glasses on at all costs, thinking marriage would fix it all. That was my downfall. That is one of the costs of childhood abuse that many people don't acknowledge – you pay the price forever, making wrong choices and always thinking you can fix things which are broken.

I found out I was pregnant with James in September 1990. He was planned and I was happy about it, although Robert wasn't. I kept Laura by me at all times, always watching for anyone showing too much interest in her, always making pacts with myself to keep her safe. We'd moved into the flat by then, which meant that Mum didn't have that much control over me, certainly not as much as she would have liked. I would go and visit her, sometimes during the day, but that is when my dad came back, around the same time as I was pregnant with James. I hadn't seen him for years but once he was back with Mum, he would visit us in the flat. They'd rekindled their relationship, which made no sense to me whatsoever. Always they'd had this awful up-and-down relationship: they'd had their battles going through the courts for custody, they had married other people, they had screamed and fought and hated each other for so long that it seemed ridiculous for them to believe they were going to have a happy ever after now.

The pregnancy was straightforward – I had to go to all the appointments on my own. I knew I had to deal with these things by myself. There's no point asking anyone when it hits you that you're on your own anyway, you just get on with it. After I had Laura, they moved the school for pregnant girls to a part of town where I'd have to do a big walk with two buses, so I only went once with Laura. By the time I was pregnant with James, no one cared that I didn't go anymore, or that I was still so young. I felt very isolated in my second pregnancy as I didn't even have that contact with school.

James' birth was straightforward and when they said it was a boy, I felt so relieved, I was crying. At this point I had no idea that abuse could happen to boys as well – I thought, *thank God, this one will be OK.* I did have post-natal depression, which I thought came from being so isolated in the flat, with no support from Robert. After I gave birth, he had a couple of days off work and I told him I needed a bit of help, but he wasn't listening. He went down to his car to go to work and I was banging on the flat window trying to get his attention. He was 13 floors down, he wouldn't hear me. I banged the window so hard, it shattered. He came back up and started bawling at me.

'What the hell is going on? Why the hell did you smash the window? Are you mental?'

'I need some help, Robert, I'm struggling. I told you that, but you never listen.'

'Oh, for fuck's sake,' he exclaimed. 'I'll get you help then.'

He told Mum and she phoned Social Services on me, which made things even worse as I felt I was being spied on and there was a pressure to act as if everything was OK to get rid of them. Overwhelmingly, there was this desperate desire not to be her, not to be my mother. If Social Services were watching me, was I on the path to becoming what I dreaded most in the world?

Life was tough. If the lifts were broken – which they usually were – I couldn't even get to the shop. I was stuck in with a toddler and a newborn all day.

The realisation that it was just me, there was no one else around to help, hit hard.

Thankfully, although I wasn't happy about it at the time, Social Services were quite good. They got Laura into a nursery, which meant I had to get up and dressed every day. Now I had a purpose. I spent the days alone with James when Laura wasn't there. We had a TV that you had to put money in, but Robert would open up the box and put the same pound through again and again. I was the one who had to deal with the TV man when he came. I'd be there with one, sometimes two, babies and the TV man would rant and rave at me: 'What the hell is going on here? Have you only had the telly on for five minutes? There's only a pound in here from the last time. Do you take me for a mug?'

'It's nothing to do with me,' I'd say, while he got angry. 'I don't have time to watch telly all day with two little 'uns needing me, do I?'

Robert used to fiddle the electricity meter as well. He did something with a cut-up cigarette box so that the meter clocked up at a different rate. I didn't like him doing these things, as he wouldn't be there to take the flak, it would be me. I'd been buying the tokens, as we could afford that, and I was trying to do it properly, but then the electric man turned up one day out of the blue. They must have suspected something as it definitely wasn't time for him to come.

'Someone's been messing with this meter,' he said, giving me a hard stare.

'I've no idea what you're talking about,' I replied, as always, not deviating from the script which had worked so far.

It looked like our luck was running out though.

'I'll have to tell my bosses about this,' he said, as fear washed over me. 'You won't get done for it but you will get charged for all the electricity you've been using.'

We ended up with a huge bill and Robert was furious, blaming me for not saying the right things rather than accepting that he'd been on the rob the whole time. He used to get really caught up in little things, becoming sure that people were out to get him, and when the matches were on at Aston Villa, he'd look out the flat window all the time, checking to see whether anyone was up to anything.

There would be kids going round saying they'd look after fans' cars for the time the match was on for a pound – but you could see them robbing them once they left! Robert was so engrossed in watching them and what they were doing. He'd be on the phone to the police, getting them to come to the football ground and round the kids up. Somehow, they found out it was him who was doing it. They graffitied the door and started threatening us, but it was just me stuck in the flat, so I got the brunt of it. I was furious with him for putting us in danger like that and it made me even more anxious and not wanting to go out at all. I hated anyone coming into my safe space and there being any confrontation as the bubble of this kind of family life kept bursting.

When the kids wrote 'grass' on the door, Robert's mum said, 'You need to move out of here.'

'Yeah, of course we do!' I told her sarcastically.

'Why don't you go to the doctor and say a man's been threatening you? Say he tried to rape you.'

'What?! Why on earth would you make up a story like that – and where did it come from? Why would I make up rubbish like that? Do you have any idea what it's like to go through anything like that and you're wanting me to make up some nonsense story?'

The abuse was always there, in the background, but I was still trying to sit on it, bury it. I thought I could lock it up forever, just keep it down and buried.

* * *

Life plodded on. I was only happy when I was with my children – the rest of the time, I was either very flat or having flashbacks. The memories of what Terry had done to me were horrendous and completely overwhelming and, in 1994, when I was 21, I asked for help and was given three free counselling sessions. The counselling was through a referral from my GP – three sessions, nothing at all really, to deal with the mental health decline I was having at this time.

The counsellor told me to write a letter to my mum to get it all out. They suggested I write the letter because, now, as a parent myself, I was very angry with her for not protecting me. I couldn't understand how she had left me so often thinking I was naughty, instead of trying to understand what was going on. I looked at my own children and just couldn't get my head around Mum not putting me first. It felt completely alien.

It wasn't to be given to Mum unless I really wanted that to happen.

I had to keep rewriting the letter as there was such a lot coming out of me, years of pent-up emotions and all the truths I'd never spoken. Mum's 40th birthday was coming up and I decided that would be it, I would build up the confidence to hand it over. I kept changing my mind but made a deal with myself that I would take it with me to her party and just see what happened, I didn't have to commit myself either way in advance.

I don't know what happened that night, maybe drinking gave me the courage, but I know I was triggered as she had a male stripper there – I thought that was absolutely disgusting. So, I gave her the letter.

'Mum, I want you read this,' I said quietly, as I

pulled her to one side and handed over the envelope with the letter that told her everything, all the abuse I'd ever been subjected to.

'Is it a birthday card?' she asked, loudly.

'Mum, you need to take this somewhere on your own and really think about what I've written down.'

She went into another room, but within minutes was back, ranting and raving. My nan and my dad were there, as was an Aunt Anna, who I was close to. Mum threw the letter at Nan, never asking if I wanted anyone else to see it, and started jabbing her finger in my face.

'What are you talking about? What are you talking about?' she yelled.

Nan was really angry with me as soon as she had read it, telling me I was a spoilt little brat looking for attention.

I'm the last person who wants attention, I try and hide, I thought. Nan wasn't impressed. My aunt sided with my nan. I left as I couldn't deal with them. To have those three women that I looked up to and should have protected me all to turn like that – well, even Mum said, 'I protected you from the ones I knew about.' They were all really dismissive. No one said, 'Let's help you – what can we do? Should we get the police involved?' No, let's push it aside was their attitude.

That night completely closed me down again and I

had to shut the lid. If they didn't believe me, well, who would? I didn't even think about the police, I had just wanted some recognition from the family. I was now in a worse position. Dad hadn't said much – I could see he was upset, but there was no conversation about it.

I was alone. Again.

18

NEW HOME, NEW LIFE

As the kids got older, my relationship with Robert grew worse. He didn't think of the impact of his actions on me and so we argued a lot. We moved in 1993 to a house in Highgate, Birmingham, a maisonette near the city centre. I had neighbours, the nursery was opposite my back gate and there was a tiny little garden. It wasn't the best area but I had people around me rather than being isolated every single day. Robert's stepdad lived in the same estate and it felt better all round, a fresh start. As always, I had my *new home, new life!* blinkers on. They didn't really work when Robert had an affair with his stepdad's neighbour.

That wasn't the worst of it. We weren't far from Cheddar Road, the red-light district, and some nights, we'd go out to a local pub with one of Robert's friends. This bloke was always saying, 'I'm not really enjoying this, I'm going to head back.' Robert would always offer to see him home safely, but I found out they were both off to Cheddar Road. Robert had been driving one night and the police brought him back, saying he had been driving under the influence, and claimed he was just sat outside waiting for his mate. But he was lying – having affairs, using prostitutes, and still having unprotected sex with me, with no regard at all.

I was just his property and he could do what he wanted. The way he talked to me was disgusting. He would say, 'Having sex with you is like the Stena Sealink – it's roll on, roll off.' Although I was a mother-of-two, I was still naïve and I accepted it all, the affairs and the prostitutes. He'd tell me it was his friend, or just a woman that was making it up. I'd say, 'OK.' I needed a perfect family so I wouldn't rock the boat.

There was more baggage too, though. All the while we lived in the maisonette, one or two of his three sisters would be living with us, so we were never alone. They were young themselves and they didn't have a good relationship with their mum. I couldn't stand that one of the girls was in a care home so I said she could stay with us. I tried to be a mum to them all, even though I was only a teenager myself.

I'd done a home-based IT course as I had plans and wanted to better myself. Also, I wanted to move and get away from Robert's mistress. For some reason – the usual reason, thinking one day everything would change and become perfect – I wanted to be back near to Mum. When we moved to Kingstanding, I went onto a government scheme of training on the job and got an NVQ III in business administration. There was a sort of 'add-on' called Managers of the Future. I was one of the first to complete the module and pass it and there was a big event at the Villa ground to signify that everyone who had succeeded had bright futures ahead of them. Clare Short MP gave out the awards and I was so proud of my achievement. Robert was bored and annoyed, getting us to leave early. What I didn't know was that there were head hunters there who had taken everyone like me aside to give them great opportunities, but I had missed that: I was bottom of the pile again.

Robert's sisters were still around and I began to work on the course, full-time, but I would come home and there wouldn't even be somewhere to sit. Robert would often meet me after work and we would go for a drink on a Friday in Birmingham. He'd do nothing but flirt with women while I sat alone. You can't deny what's in front of your face, no matter how naïve you are.

No matter what was going on, my blinkers always

seemed to be firmly in place though. I decided that if we got married, it would be OK – it would all be OK. In between me asking him to marry me (of course I was the one to propose) and the actual wedding date, Robert started stopping out at night. A good friend of his was in the Army and came back sometimes, just to see Robert really, and they would stay out all night together. I'd be phoning hospitals and everything, police stations even, and he'd come back in the morning, saying there had been some trouble and they'd got taken to another station I hadn't called – it was all absolute rubbish.

I'd asked him to get his sisters to stay in line a bit and that made him furious. Any time I brought it up, he'd get so angry, culminating one night in him throwing glass across the room, which cut the top of my head open. There was blood everywhere. I was due to go and have a bridal hair trial a couple of days later and had to have bits cut off due to the injury. I felt I had to go through with it as it was all booked, everyone was expecting it. Lots of women experience domestic abuse when they are married, but I had so much abuse at such an important point of my childhood to deal with as well. The knock-on effect for all of your life is huge. Your boundaries have been smashed from a very young age, people can do what they want to you and then they only have to show you a tiny bit of affection or niceness and you fall for it. That stays on repeat. Robert could be as horrible as he wanted and he just had to show a tiny bit of kindness now and again to make me stay. He would also use my abuse against me and said I deserved it and he could understand how it had happened.

'Look at you, you're a mess,' was his mantra.

I had felt able to open up to him but when he threw my abuse back at me, it was a dagger. I thought he was probably right, though – my self-esteem was smashed.

'You'll turn out like your mum,' he'd say horribly. 'I'll be off down the road if you start looking like that.' I was always slim, I had the tiniest bit of weight from the babies but I was thin anyway. I became bulimic, thinking he would leave me if I put weight on. It went on for a year. I would eat so much, then purge myself when no one was there, apart from the kids. I would stuff myself with lots of rubbish food – biscuits, bread, everything I could get my hands on. I had a plan, I knew what I was going to do every single time. Mostly it would be after Laura was off to nursery and James was settled down. I would make an omelette with mixed veg out of a tin, quick and easy, but it was also something I ate back when I was a kid, so perhaps it was comforting. I'd add chocolate and biscuits – and I'd put salad on the side for some reason, even though I'd just be throwing it all up again, knowing I could eat as much as I wanted.

I feel different houses were different symbols in my life. It's like you completely reinvent yourself each time you move and in 1997, we moved again. Every time I moved, I could have my dream again, telling myself it was the house or the area rather than looking at the fact that it was another abusive episode. Shortly after we married, we bought a house but it was literally over the road from Robert's sisters. It wasn't a fresh start at all. I hated that house from the start: all the same issues were there, he was still the same, his sisters were still there.

I got pregnant in that house – another fresh start. I did the place out lovely, all clean and perfect for more kids, but became really ill early on, with stomach cramps so bad that I couldn't get out of bed. I miscarried, but I found out I was still pregnant so it must have been twins – sadly, I lost the other one too. I got pregnant again not long after that and had another miscarriage. Robert didn't seem to care in the slightest, he didn't miss a beat.

I had moved to a job at Nationwide Cables just after I married, in September 1997. It was supposed to be the best day of my life, but it was miles away from that. Mum, Dad, my brother, Robert's sisters and his mum were all there as well as a few friends. It was a lavish do in a posh hotel in Birmingham, but it was awful. It was all about the show and not the reality I was feeling, having had my head cut by the glass only recently. Robert arrived after me and when he saw me with my hair up and curled, he said I looked like I'd been dragged through a hedge backwards. Not the words you want to hear from your groom at the altar. He was the sort of person who joked about everything, you could rarely have a deep and meaningful conversation with him. I had to brush this off too, even though it cut deep.

After the ceremony, we took the photos, then headed over to the venue, which was a short walk away. There was a red carpet rolled out and I felt like I could now relax and try to enjoy the day. But it wasn't to be. When the wedding song started up, Robert was nowhere to be found. They had to stop it and send people to look for him. He was found in the women's loo, chatting up female wedding guests. It was the final insult.

The evening went on and I just couldn't wait to go to bed. When I woke up in the morning, I couldn't stop crying – I felt as if I had made one of the worst mistakes of my life.

At Nationwide Cables I was working with my childhood friend Kelly and it felt so nice to be with other women. They were a fantastic support network and helped me to see that my treatment at the hands of Robert just wasn't right. Standing by the coffee machine, having a fag, I would see their reactions when we all talked.

'What are you doing, putting up with all that?' one of them asked me and it was like a light going on. I'd never had that before. It cleared everything for me and I saw it wasn't normal. If you've never heard that before, in a family that has no morals, no boundaries, where anything goes, to be outside that bubble for a bit with other women to bounce off can change things. That community of women gave me strength.

I knew it wasn't good for the kids to be there too – they couldn't be around that sort of relationship. One night, I had gone out with women from work. My relationship was so strained by then as Robert hadn't helped me through any of the miscarriages and I knew he was with other women all the time. I'd given up all hope of it being a lovely marriage. I was getting sound advice now, telling me I didn't need to put up with it. That night, Robert turned up for some reason. I was actually dancing, having a great time, and he saw me and went ballistic, dragging me out of the club and throwing me into the gutter.

'When I met you, I got you out of the gutter and that's where I'll leave you.'

The bouncers had seen him, as had other people

outside. They came over and checked I was OK, then they took him round the corner and beat him up – it was probably the first time he'd faced any consequences. I got a taxi as he'd pushed me so hard on the ground that he had chipped my coccyx. I decided to go to my mum's as I was in such pain that I could hardly walk and she took me to A&E. I stayed with her for a couple of days to get my head together and all the questions started bubbling up: what was I doing, where should I go from here? I went back, got the kids and left. This time I would try to do it on my own, this time I would stay strong.

***

We split up 18 months after we married and we were only together that long because I thought of myself as dirt on his shoe. I found myself back home again with my mum and dad – they had bought a house together in West Bromwich by then. They were both working and seemed to have things sorted. It only had two bedrooms so I rented a private house nearby with the kids quite quickly.

When I left Robert, I was working in sales. The company had 250 national branches, where people phoned in with their sales every day, and I got to know some of them really well. They ended up telling me all their problems – it's like when Gavin and Stacey first met! I was chatting to lots of people I got on well with, but one man – Phil, from Manchester – was very friendly and I told him what was going on in my life. Very quickly, I was in a relationship with him – I was about 26 by then, in 1999.

I'd been with Robert for 11 years and I can see, looking back, that I had a pattern of always falling into relationships very quickly. I find myself love bombed, in a relationship before I've even decided I want to be in that relationship – it takes a certain type of man to do that and they seek out women who will be susceptible to it. The men in my life have always been really outspoken and overpowering to the point of being narcissistic – do I attract them or do they attract me, I wonder.

With Phil living in Manchester, his location was really good for me as it became another of my coping mechanisms – I liked him living far away. I'd see him when the kids went to their dad at the weekends; I could keep my family separate, I was back to putting things in boxes. My head was full of what I was carrying, it felt like I was exploding, but I had the *fresh start* belief I always clung to. Here was another one – everything would be fine.

The kids would have a weekend with their dad while Phil would come and pick me up, taking me back to Manchester with him. It felt like I could breathe for a little bit. He was lovely actually, one of the nicest people I've ever met, and I don't think he was a narcissist. I think maybe because I had met him on the phone, not in real life, it worked better – I knew his personality before I met him. I'd have a couple of days in Manchester but when I came back, the overload made me wonder if it was worth it. It was a respite for me but then I returned to reality, to normal life, and it was all too much. I decided that it wasn't working with Phil after about six months and that we should just stay friends, which was actually one of the only times in my life something had worked out with a man.

I was on my own in the new house with the two kids, but Robert was in and out all the time, making drama. On Sundays, Dad and I would go out and watch live bands together. I loved that, it was our thing. Mum would be making Sunday dinner and she'd look after the kids while we went out. It's so weird, that contrast, as she was the perfect nan to them, despite being an awful mother to me. She would read with them, take them on holidays, all sorts of nice things, and they have no bad memories of her growing up at all. After the initial fight with her, I initiated contact again. I was alone in a flat with two young children and I needed my mum. I always had, even if she didn't have much to offer me. I didn't know any different at this stage – I would take any crumb she offered, even if that crumb was poisonous.

When Robert had attacked me outside the club, I got a taxi to my mum's. I stayed with her for a few days once I left A&E. The kids stayed with Robert and his sisters, who lived over the road. I was completely broken at this point. I'd not long had a second miscarriage and was now facing this. I deeply regret leaving the kids with him because he used the time to tell them that their mum had abandoned them, really messing with their heads. Laura found this especially difficult. The reality was I'd been so beaten down by his infidelity, his constant put downs and his lack of support with the miscarriages, my confidence and self-esteem were at rock bottom. I could barely look after myself, so I had to take a few days headspace to decide what I was going to do, how I could find a new home and plan a life for just me and the kids.

When Mum and Dad got back together in 1991, it felt like I had a proper family for once. The kids had a nan and grandad like other kids. They were both great with Laura and James. It was like Mum had a second chance with them, to be a better person than she had ever been with me. They moved to West Bromwich, where they both had jobs, and appeared settled. I started to trust her with the kids, even allowing them both to take them on holidays to Butlin's. It was what I had always wanted and needed from Mum, for her to be attentive. I knew she hadn't been with me, but I would settle for her being good with my children.

I enjoyed moments of light with Dad when we went out on Sundays, too. It was just enough to keep me going. Two kids alone, trying to work, hardly any money, Robert creating drama, but my dad was a respite on those afternoons. He had a friend, Pete, who used to come along too. I suppose I was getting on with Pete, building up a non-physical relationship with him, until after a year or so, Dad went home early one evening.

'I've had enough,' he said. 'I think I'll have an early night.'

'Stay and have a drink with me, Della,' Pete said.

So I did and that night, he came back to mine. We sat up all night just talking rubbish but it was nice, we got on. We arranged another date but Dad was protective by then, so we decided not to tell him and see how it went first.

During that week, I got a phone call from my mum.

'He's been shot! He's been shot!' she was screaming.

'What are you on about?' I tried to get some sense out of her but she was hysterical. 'Dad's been shot? How? Where?'

She was sobbing and screeching until she finally

managed to string a sentence together: 'Christ, it's not your dad, Della – it's Pete.'

I could hardly take it in. Pete and my dad were like Laurel and Hardy – Dad was short and tubby, Pete was lanky and 6ft 7in. Walking down the High Street, you could tell them a mile off. They were walking down the road after being at the pub the night before Mum called and some lads walked past, one of them barging my dad.

'What d'you think you're doing?' asked Pete. 'How rude.'

There was a bang.

Dad thought a firework had been let off, but it was a gun: one of them had shot Pete.

Things quickly became unreal, it was like living in a movie. It was chaos for a while. Very quickly, even though we hadn't decided we might try for a relationship, Pete and I were thrown into something. I went to see him a lot in hospital and when he came out, somehow it just seemed to be decided that he would come to mine for me to look after. Again, it wasn't a choice I made – it just happened.

The police were obviously heavily involved and we had a police liaison officer visit us too.

'He needs to move out of West Brom,' they said when they found out it was a gang from London. 'They know where he lives and he needs police protection. He's seen their faces, he can identify them.'

It all meant that I never really had the chance to say I wanted to be in a relationship with this man, it was just a case of us all needing to move. It was such an upheaval for the kids, Laura was about 11 and James 10, to a new house, with a new man in their life, and my daughter went completely off the rails. I didn't seem to be involved in my own life. I only knew Pete from going out with Dad, we'd never even slept together. I'd been to hospital, seen what he had gone through, met his family and it all just became a case of me wanting to help him through this traumatic event. Repairing any part of myself was on the backburner again: we were moving, contacting new schools, with none of us knowing anyone – another fresh start? Even I was beginning to feel that was unlikely.

19

STUCK

After six months, I saw the real side of Pete. He turned out to be an alcoholic, with a gambling problem. His family all knew this, but they are all like Hyacinth Bucket from *Keeping Up Appearances* – everything is fantastic on the surface, but peep behind the curtain... Pete never had to take responsibility for his actions. I think they were glad that I'd taken him off their hands. Pete was far too keen on trying to discipline my kids the 'old-fashioned way'. There wasn't a chance of that happening so we were in constant conflict. Things had calmed down with Robert as he had a new, very young girlfriend, but he wasn't even allowed to park on the drive by Pete when he collected the kids. It wasn't explicit control but he did it in subtle ways: he'd make dinner, but only for me and him, not for the kids.

'What are the kids going to eat?' I'd say, looking at our steak.

'Don't know, don't care,' he'd reply.

Within those six months, I knew that I had to get out. I went to a solicitor and explained what had been going on and she told me, 'This is domestic abuse, Della.'

'No, he doesn't hit me,' I said. 'He's never tried that.'

'It doesn't have to be hitting,' she told me. 'Look at how he's trying to control the kids, wanting to discipline them. You've said that he never knows when he's drunk because he drinks so much. He sounds like a functioning alcoholic to me, he's gambling all of the household money. He's driven and has built businesses, but he spends every penny he gets as soon as it's in his pocket. That's financial abuse, you get the scraps.'

She was right and other things clicked into place. If I was on the phone to Robert, he'd take it out of my hand.

'Come near my house and there'll be a hammer waiting for you,' he'd snarl.

'You need to get out,' the solicitor said. 'We can get injunctions in place.'

I went home and told his family they needed to pick him up.

'Your kids need discipline,' said Mum. 'He's the best thing that ever happened to you, don't mess it up.

He's working, you've got a roof over your head. You need to appreciate what you've got, Della.'

No one was listening to me. Over the next days and weeks, Pete's parents kept coming round and crying, begging me to keep him. I just thought again that no one was listening, my needs were at the bottom of the pile again.

I took an overdose, I just couldn't cope. I'd been given tablets to help me stop smoking, but they gave me nightmares, which meant I'd stopped. It also meant that I had plenty of them. I collected them all, as well as my antidepressants, which I'd only been on for a few weeks, anything I could get my hands on. It had all built up and I just couldn't go on. I felt that Laura hated me, she would sit up banging on my bedroom door at night, she was completely wild and to me, it was like a symbol that I had nothing I could control in my life, nothing I could make good. I had been to Social Services and asked for help with her and they had ignored it, school had ignored it. Pete's parents were begging me to keep him, Mum was telling me that I was lucky – was it any wonder that it all came to a head one night?

I locked myself in the bathroom with a bottle of vodka and took the tablets, all of them.

I don't remember the next few days. I was in hospital, but that's all I know.

I had wanted to protect my kids since the day they were born, but I had been brought to this. You think everyone will be better off when you're lost in a situation like that. The kids would go to Robert and that would be fine. No one would miss me and the pain would be over. Some people think it's selfish, but you get to a point where you are so exhausted, there is no one helping you and you just want everything to stop. You don't want to end your life, you don't want to die, you just want a rest. When I looked back, so many bad things had happened – I thought, *if this is what life is, I don't want it. There had been no respite. If this is the next 30 years, I don't want to bother.*

Pete and Laura found me, but I don't know the details – it breaks my heart that my little girl saw her own mother like that. That's the worst thing of all. From the moment I found out Laura had been there, I promised I would never do it again. It's been a hard promise to keep, but I have.

They found me in the morning, unconscious. I got rushed to hospital and woke up three days later. It's just awful to think there are three whole days I can't remember and I imagine what everyone was going through, while I lay there.

It was the worst and the best thing I'd ever done. Afterwards, the school helped, Social Services came, I did get support. It was all because of the suicide attempt though, they wouldn't have done it otherwise. I went back home after those three days and for the first time, people were on my side. Pete and his family were really good. The worst thing ever had galvanised some action but the truth was, I'd been shouting for years. It shouldn't have got that far.

I got sent for a psychiatric assessment but the doctor was on another planet. I explained everything to him, how I had got to that point, and he looked at me as if he couldn't understand a word of it. He just kept saying I would be on the Psychiatric Register for ten years and after an hour, that was the end of my time with him. What I needed was some understanding, an acknowledgement of it all, to be seen for the first time. I might as well have been asking for the moon.

Sadly, it didn't take long for people to just slip into how they had been before. I was expected to go back to what I had always been for other people, although I was thankful that Laura did get the help she was crying out for. Pete stopped laying down the law and had to go to family sessions with Robert. Those family sessions were supposed to be for Laura, for us all to understand what she was going through with the upheaval, but Pete made them all about him, so nothing was really resolved. All of this had affected James too, but boys tend to handle things very differently and he wasn't as vocal as Laura.

I could see now that I'd almost been duped into the relationship with Pete. I didn't really ever have a chance to decide whether I wanted to be with him or not. There was little planning about the next stage of my life either and I got pregnant with my son Charlie quite soon. I had him in October 2002, just a year after my suicide attempt. It was Charlie's birth that brought on severe PTSD (post-traumatic stress disorder). He had to be induced and I think that contributed a great deal to it, as someone else was taking control, things were being done to me and my body. I had a sweep to try and bring on labour – a very invasive process, which shocked me. The sensation of someone doing that, invading me, felt like I was being taken back to those years with Terry. I was sent away and told to come back the next day for another invasive process. When that didn't work and the midwife team wanted to do more, I'd had enough.

'No, you're not doing anything to me again.'

Luckily, the contractions soon started. Because of the pessary I'd had to induce labour, there wasn't the normal, gradual build-up I'd had with my other two children. Your body is doing what it needs to do then, but once the pessaries and induction take over, control goes. I was never told it would be zero to 100mph like that, I was taken to the delivery suite at 4cm and hooked up to a monitor so that they could turn my contractions up and down. All of the control was taken away from me. It was horrendous. I felt myself dissociating and going into myself, getting flashbacks. I couldn't communicate with the people in the room and I couldn't tell anyone what was happening. I was flashing back to being raped, to Terry doing those things and saying, 'You deserve it, you're a disgusting little bitch.'

I was in a situation which is supposed to be the most beautiful experience, bringing a new life into the world, but I was overwhelmed with my past and couldn't tell anyone. After Charlie came out, I didn't come round for half an hour. I wasn't aware of him being born. I've lost that, it's hard to accept. Midwives and obstetricians need to be trained in trauma, but when you dissociate, people just don't understand. If even one of that team had been trauma informed, they could have seen the signs, seen that I wasn't interacting, seen that I wasn't even aware I'd given birth. I don't even remember holding Charlie while everyone else did – I was just flat, not aware of anything.

I'd never experienced flashbacks or dissociation as intense as that before – and to think of it when I was giving birth was horrific. Maybe trying to kill myself had made me even more raw as that whole episode had opened up a big hole I couldn't ignore. Everything could become overwhelming very easily. I had learned to put things in boxes and shut doors on things, but the suicide was the stage where the doors flung open and I was unable to box it all up. I was starting to realise how my past abuse was affecting relationships with my family. I looked at my daughter, watching what was going on, starting to suffer herself. I had felt that as long as they were OK, I could pay the price, but once it started affecting my kids ... And Charlie had been born into that.

I was straight back into life with a new baby and feeling the intense desperation to protect him. Most mums feel that, of course, but this really was intense. I always had the idea that if I got them to 18, I would have done it, but that's naïve, isn't it? It's particularly naive with girls as the fear for them is for life. Everywhere you look, there are threats, there are men who want to hurt them. That never goes – a woman can never sit back and think *I'm safe now*. I know there will be some who say men go through that too, men are killed in higher numbers, men can be victims – I would say that might be true, but we have an epidemic of violence and hatred towards women and girls, and as a mother, the fear of that always being there made my blood run cold.

I was also terrified that because the dissociation had happened at such an intense point with the birth, it might start happening more. And that had been such a small amount of memories – what if everything came back at once? I wouldn't be able to cope with it and I wouldn't be there to protect my children. As much as I thought, *that was bad*, I knew there was more to come. I battle with that to this day as I know there are memories I haven't dealt with yet. It was a constant battle between the me I wanted to be and the me of my past.

Things on the surface were very different to the battle below. I told no one about dissociating – I don't think anyone would have understood it. I had been fighting for years, a silent battle, and after the suicide attempt, I was sent to that unhelpful psychiatrist who made me think I had to put it in a box again. Where could I go, what could I do?

I was supposed to go back to work after Charlie's birth but just didn't feel able to. I lost all of the support from the women I had built up relationships with as I never went back and that was a big deal. There is something about a community of women that offers unique support as they all share their problems in a completely open way and you get a sense of what's right and what's wrong. Until Charlie was two, it was pretty much just me and him. Laura and James were old enough to be sorting themselves out, so it should have been quite easy just looking after one, but I was trying to put a lid on my past very badly. I was just getting through. I had that constant fear every day that this could be the day it could all go wrong.

Practical pressures did start to tail off a bit – Pete began doing well in his business and Mum won the lottery. She was in a ten-person syndicate that won £1.9 million. She gave me £10k, although she told everyone it was a lot more than that. Life felt as if it had a sort of even keel and we even went on holiday to Turkey with Mum and Dad on Charlie's second birthday. I didn't enjoy it that much, but had no idea what was really going on – my head was like mush.

As Pete's business was doing well, we went on more trips. We took the kids to Canada for Christmas, starting off in Toronto, seeing the Niagara Falls, then renting a house in the middle of nowhere that had massive bows on it like something out of a fairy tale. We came back after a long trip which had refreshed me a bit, but were soon straight into family upheaval. That year, Mum and Dad split up and she moved to Turkey. It was as much a shock to Dad as it was to everyone else.

One of the people in the lottery with Mum owned a café with a Turkish man. Before our family trip, Mum had gone to see this friend and when we all went, it was clear that she was planting the seeds for something else. She was distracted all the time and didn't really engage.

One of his friends said to him one day, 'I didn't realise you were selling your house, Arthur.' Neither did he! It was in the window of the estate agent and he had no idea. Mum had gone on holiday to Turkey by herself, come back quite quickly, then started things in motion to get the house on the market as she'd met someone when she was there. Dad thought she was having an affair in West Brom before she left, but she swore blind she wasn't – however, she did have someone in Turkey.

Charlie was four by then and we continued to travel when we could, going to Australia and New Zealand. I would feel lighter as soon as the plane took off, as if all my worries were being left behind. As soon as it landed on the way back, the old fears and the trauma were back.

We bought our council house too, but at that point, you could still get loans at ridiculous levels. We got a mortgage for 125 per cent, which was so dangerous, however Pete was always one for taking risks. The relationship wasn't great still but the holidays were papering over the cracks. The time we spent together in New Zealand showed that it was a rotten relationship. He was constantly nagging Laura and James, telling them that they had no manners, that they didn't appreciate things – he wanted a show of them being so grateful to him. We argued a lot and decided to split when we got back, but then I found out I was pregnant with Ellie.

Everything fell to pieces after that as I had the same birth experience, but it wasn't just the delivery this time, it was the whole pregnancy. I had flashbacks, I was dissociating. Again, I had an induced labour and again, I felt as if other people were taking over my body. When I was about to start pushing, the curtain around me was pushed open and Pete's mum waltzed in. I was gone by then, completely out of my own body, but it was one of the most intimate positions I could have been in and I was violated again.

It took a while to come back to the world again after Ellie was born, but there was also a terror when I got home. I couldn't sleep, I couldn't stop crying, the flashbacks wouldn't stop this time. Ellie was born in July 2006 and I was suicidal by Christmas. I could see Terry, I could feel it all again, as if he was actually there with me. It was like the bottom of my world had fallen out, I just couldn't stop the flashbacks or see that it was worth carrying on. Not only had I gone through so much abuse as a child, I was having to relive it as an adult. I couldn't switch it off, I couldn't put it in a box. This would be my existence forever.

Terry Price had given me a life sentence.

20

HELP ME

In December 2006, I felt like I couldn't go on without something changing. I searched and searched for someone, somewhere, who could help, finally settling on a group called Rugby RoSA, a local charity for survivors of rape and sexual abuse.

I wrote to them and said: 'I am an adult survivor of child abuse and have finally come to a point in my life where I want to confront my demons head on and put them away once and for all. I have managed very well up until now – but every time I have a new baby, all the memories come flooding back and start to take over my life again. This first happened 17 years ago when I had my first and second child, then again it started up after my third child four years ago. Again, I managed to push it to the back of my mind, but now having had my fourth child, I am in its grasp again. This is it now – I can't let it take over anymore, I want to get my life back. My way of coping up until now is to spend like there is no tomorrow, and for this, my family is suffering greatly. I have bills and debt collectors chasing me every day, I feel like I just want to run away.'

The spending had been an issue for a while and it didn't take much to figure out that my need for material possessions was a direct link from when Terry Price had said he would buy me things in exchange for abusing me. I thought it was the only way to show I was worth something – I had to break that cycle.

My debt was crippling, all from catalogues and online shopping. Most people understand that survivors can develop drug and alcohol addictions as coping mechanisms in response to their trauma, but many don't realise that spending is also another addiction and way of coping. I suppose in my case this is related to being promised 'things' in return for not talking about what was being done to me. I would make sure my kids wanted for nothing and if that meant me being in debt, then it was worth it. They would never be in a position of having to give something of themselves in return for putting up with abuse. My kids would have the best of everything at whatever cost to me.

They got back to me by the next morning, offering to find me help and an assessment, which was organised very quickly. I was desperately hoping that something could be in place to help me get through Christmas. In floods of tears, I could hardly express what was going on: 'I'm just a mess,' I kept saying, over and over. The initial counsellor was fantastic, giving me a one-hour session in which she could see how bad things were. They quickly arranged for me to see someone in Coventry and I got the bus there with Ellie in the pram. I saw a trainee therapist, but she was a lifesaver, I don't know what I would have done without that safe space to tell my story. She taught me about CBT (cognitive behavioural therapy), which helped with where I was at that point, rather than addressing the trauma, but I really had to look into myself. It made me deal with the here and now, with my relationship and my working life; it made me look at what I wanted to do with my life.

So much came out very quickly. After each session, I was given tasks and the questions would make it obvious to me that I had a number of unhealthy patterns. I kept myself ridiculously busy so that I rarely had time to think about myself, because when I did, the past would come back to haunt me. It also became clear that I had a lot of anger, even if I didn't show it. I wasn't allowed to grow up freely and experience a normal childhood – I'll never know what the real me should have been.

The counselling made me realise that I wanted Pete out of my life. One night, Laura offered to look after Charlie and Ellie for me if I needed a break to see a friend for coffee and a chat. She dropped me there and Charlie fell asleep in his car seat on the way back. Laura picked him up, took him indoors and put him at the bottom of the stairs so she could go back and get everything else out of the car. Pete knew the relationship was at breaking point by then and that night, he exploded. He came out into the hallway and was screaming at Laura about leaving Charlie.

'I literally just put him down to go back to the car!' she said. 'I'd never put him in any danger, you know that.' Pete followed her out and was aggressive, slamming the car door on her arm and trying to have a go at her partner. It was awful and I wasn't there to stop any of it. Laura phoned me, hysterical, and I said, 'Get the police.' They had to remove Pete from the house, which was awful for Charlie to see. Pete blamed it all on Laura and even went so far as to coach Charlie, so that his and Laura's close relationship was now in tatters too.

Going for CBT gave me the strength to know the relationship was no good, none of this was any good – once Pete did that to Laura, I knew that was it, he needed to leave. The police did help with that and the CBT helped too, because I had to look at the here and now with my relationship and what I wanted out of life. However, I did have to be the big, strong mum again and sort everything out, which allowed me to put things in boxes as I had to deal with life. It wasn't dealing with any trauma at all.

At the end of the sessions, I felt like I had some sort of idea of where my life was going and one thing I wanted was to go to university. Life was hard as Pete wouldn't pay the bills and I was being threatened with court by the mortgage company. We were soon made homeless and were given an awful council house in 2008.

The counselling went on for about five months. I felt like I was having a mental breakdown. During my sessions, they asked if I would like to formally report the sexual abuse offences and that someone from their office would be there to support me if I did. I thought long and hard about it, as I had many times over the years, and concluded yes, now was the time. I'd do it, I *could* do it, if someone was with me. They made arrangements for the police to come to the house with one of the counsellors there for support. On the day, they said there was no counsellor available but the police already had a time slot to come. Did I want to go ahead? Yes, it was now or never and if I didn't, I would probably never be ready again.

Two male police officers turned up and I was overwhelmed. I couldn't go into detail. This was the hardest thing I have ever had to do on my own, especially as it was male officers they sent out and they had already been made fully aware of what I would be disclosing. They weren't great at listening, especially with my report of abuse being what they called 'historic'. They took some notes but when they realised where it had happened, told me that they couldn't really deal with it anyway as it was another force. It felt like a dead end.

When it was over, I was drained. I hadn't wanted to disclose my past to male officers and I hadn't wanted to do so without someone from the charity there. However, I had, I'd managed it, and now I just had to sit back and wait for someone to contact me. I don't think I can emphasise how much you need to have promises met, plans upheld, in that situation. It's what you hold onto. You've given away your story and you need someone to stick with it, to do what they said they'll do, and for things to progress at their end while you live with this burning ball of anxiety inside you.

Every day was met with a hope that I'd hear from West Midlands Police. Nothing happened for ages and I finally plucked up the courage to contact the original officers and ask what was going on. They had no idea, they didn't seem to think it was any sort of priority, but they did say they would chase it up when they could. I left it in their hands, there was nothing else I could do.

I left it in their hands for seven years and they didn't say a word to me.

***

In that time, everything was put away again in my mind, with me hoping for nothing more than my kids to be safe. I just wanted a normal life, to provide for them, to have a career. I had gone to a local volunteer centre to try and open a door into doing something to help me find a focus in my life and that's where I saw the leaflet for a 2+2 degree – two years at a local college with the last two years at Warwick University. I could just about manage at college as I had to complete about 120 units over two years, but when I went to university, it changed to 120 units per year. I'd got through by the skin of my teeth, but it was so much more with a 40-minute drive each way, a massive university on a spread-out campus in its own little world. I felt like a fish out of water with all those young people. The coursework and reading were now double and it was overwhelming. I'd get there and get a call about the kids, and I started to wonder why I was trying so hard, killing myself to do it with no support.

Who was I trying to prove something to anyway?

The course itself was smacking me in the face – the sociology, the politics – telling me how bad the world was. I would rather have lived in ignorance. Trying to juggle too much, I was falling into depression again. I know I was clever enough, but all of the other pressures were in my way. It was demoralising to think that if I hadn't had the life I'd had, I would be someone else.

Ellie was unwell at that point too. It turned out she was coeliac but that took a while to diagnose. She had water infections, ridiculous temperatures, sickness, diarrhoea and she would just sleep all day in the corner at nursery. No doctor was listening to me and I begged for years. I gave up university in December 2009. Why would I ever get something I wanted after all? I was resigned to it: no matter how hard I tried, I would always be treading water – it was like snakes and ladders and I'd never get to the top.

After Mum won the lottery and went to Turkey in 2003, we had very little contact as she'd decided that I had taken sides with my dad and didn't want anything to do with me. However, in 2007, she started emailing again. She had bought a flat in Turkey but, according to her, it belonged to the Turkish Mafia and they were now after her. Mum's stories were getting weirder and more wonderful as the years went on.

She said she was in debt to the Mafia and needed the cash she had given me back to pay them off. I'd already given her a fair bit of money to come back for her dad's funeral – although she never did bother attending and stayed in Turkey when she should have been here in the UK.

In 2007, when I'd just had Ellie, out of nowhere Mum claimed she was pregnant too – which was pretty odd given she'd gone through the menopause before she left!

'I've had IVF,' she said.

'You've done what?'

I didn't believe a word of it, but she kept saying it was true and calling me all the names under the sun for questioning this miracle conception. There wasn't a huge amount of contact between us still as I couldn't be bothered with all her wild stories and she couldn't be bothered with the fact that I didn't believe them. However, one day, she turned up at my door, completely out of the blue. She'd been a big woman the last time I'd seen her but now she was so thin, there was nothing to her.

'I need this money,' she said. 'I've just had twins. You need to give me cash or I don't know what I'll do.'

'Mum, you're skinny as a rake! How could you just have had twins? Where are they if you did?'

'They're in intensive care.'

Her phone went off and she ignored it.

'Don't you want to answer that?' I asked.

'No, no, I don't.'

'Who is it?'

'It's none of your business, that's who it is.'

It was a stand-off.

'If you must know, it's Ali – my partner.'

'Shouldn't you answer it then? After all, it might be about … the twins.'

She kept staring me down. Every time the phone rang, she ignored it.

'Look, Mum, if you've really had a baby – *two* babies – then surely you should be answering a call from Turkey if they're in intensive care over there?'

'Don't you tell me what to do – if you cared at all, you'd just give me the money and I'd leave you alone.'

'I don't *have* the money, Mum! You gave me that as a gift and you've been asking me for it back almost since the moment I got it. You know that I've spent it, on the house and getting us sorted for Ellie coming, and I sent you lots when Grandad died …'

'I'm not here for excuses, I'm here to get my money.'

The phone was going constantly.

'You need to leave – get out of my house! If you want to meet and talk, I'll do that, but not here.'

She left, with no commitment to meet again, but I was told she spent the rest of her time in the UK shopping, mostly for bikinis and dresses. Not really the actions of a woman who had just given birth to twins who were in intensive care. She went back and I got word that she wanted a Skype with me. I agreed to it, and as soon as she came on screen, I could see a man in the background. Apparently one of the twins had died by this point. She was pulling on my heartstrings as a mother because I kept thinking, *what if it's true?* It sounded ridiculous, but what if? She was sat there pouring her heart out and she had one, really fat baby sat on her lap. It certainly didn't look premature.

'I need this money – we have to live in a tent in the middle of the desert unless I pay people off.'

She said the other baby had died of respiratory issues but she was sitting there with the other child on her lap and she was smoking constantly.

'I don't have the money, but come home. I can put a roof over your head, I can feed you, but I can't physically send you more money.'

This man was getting really angry in the background and was obviously telling her what to say. I felt sorry for her again as she was clearly under duress and he was making her do whatever he wanted.

'I can't come back – the laws are different over here and the man gets the child and I'd lose her. I'm an illegal immigrant. If I tell anyone, they'll kick me out.'

'Isn't that what you want? Wouldn't that mean you could get away from him? With the child?'

'It doesn't work that way – you don't understand anything.'

'Can't you go to the British Embassy?'

I got an email: *You've never been there for me. You're a terrible person. I don't see why you can't just send me money and help me – you do know I'll have to kill myself and my daughter to get away from these people? There's nothing else for me. And it'll all be your fault …*

I replied and said, 'You can't keep doing this to me. It's emotionally abusive. Just stop. I've told you what you need to do. You need to take responsibility, come back here and I'll help you.' I didn't get a reply.

One day, I was walking Ellie to school, looking at the ducks in the local pond, and she wanted to get in the river beside them, with Charlie, on the trip back home. When we got back, Pete's parents were outside and I instantly thought something was wrong. She had come to tell me that Mum was back and that she'd been to hers.

'She doesn't look right – you need to see her.'

'She wants money, doesn't she?'

'She does, but she needs it, Della.'

'How much is she saying I owe her now?'

'Forty thousand pounds.'

'God, it's getting bigger with every story she tells. I'll show you what she gave me and how much she's had back from me. I haven't got any more but I've said so many times that she can come stay and I'll feed her.'

That's how I knew she was back in the country.

'Well, here's her number ...'

'I can't call it – every time she says anything to me, it puts me back in an emotional state that I'm a kid again. I have my own children to look after.'

Laura was against that – she had been a good nan to her and James, and they'd never seen the bad side of her before she dumped everyone to go to Turkey. 'You should call her,' Laura said. 'She might need you.'

'You call her if you like, but be aware, she will manipulate you. She's just after money.'

Laura texted her and quickly realised that was the truth. She was asking for money within a few messages. She wasn't interested in Freya, Laura's daughter, or what they had been through.

Right. Well, I'm in a flat with nothing, no white goods, nothing. Can you help me out?

I'd warned her that would happen and Laura said she could take her round charity shops, but she wasn't interested. My whole world was becoming so overwhelming, my mind felt like it would explode.

One thing I had learned from my time at university was about PTSD. Until that point, I'd only ever heard of it in relation to soldiers. I didn't know it was a trauma response. Suddenly, it started to make sense. I had been in a war zone, I had been in survival mode, for years. Soldiers get to come home – I'd had no break. There was no one traumatic incident, it was one after another which had resulted in complex PTSD. That knowledge should have been a call to arms for me, but I do this thing of reinventing myself – closing doors, opening new ones – and I was still in that loop. I thought I needed to do something for me, something I wanted.

It was the days of MySpace and there was a man I used to follow called The Music Man. He promoted a lot of unsigned bands and created a really nice community, where people just chatted about music. I got to know a few people in music journalism and I set up a group called Midland Music Maniacs. I had space for ten unsigned bands each month and I would scour the internet for gigs, radio slots, festival slots and post out the opportunities for the bands. It became really busy with bands contacting me and a waiting list for them to be featured. Radio stations were following my page as well.

I was reclaiming music, something I had lost from such a young age. I needed a website built and I started having people go out to different gigs for me, reviewers and photographers. I started having a bit of a social life then as I could go out to the gigs too and even build up friendships. It was a lovely network. I had developed it from nothing to the stage where one of my reviewers started up our own radio show and even sold advertising on the website – this was my new clean slate. It was my escape.

It was also my way of masking things as I would drink a lot by then. I'd been drinking since I was 12 or 13, but now it was masking everything. I was getting to the stage where I was having blackouts and it was getting dangerous. One of the last festivals I went to in 2014, getting ready to watch a band in the afternoon, I don't remember anything else after until 11pm. I woke up and there were bright lights everywhere. I thought I'd died, but I was actually in the medical tent. That was a reality check – *what the hell are you doing, Della?* I asked myself. It was the final straw – I was the one person responsible for two little kids at home, who Laura was looking after for me. I stopped, but that was the end to the music journey too.

I lost the love and energy for something I had built up from nothing, which became another snake I'd slid down. Laura had given birth to my first grandchild Freya in 2011 and at 11 days old, she was rushed to intensive care. It was touch and go, and I just wanted to fix everything for my family. It turned out that Freya had a twisted bowel; she was operated on and had to stay in hospital for six weeks. I had to focus on them. In 2014, I started doing a bit of volunteering again, working with newly released offenders (never sex offenders). I was always trying to help other people rather than myself; I wanted to fix things for them. I'd get them settled into accommodation, give them a pack of basics, get their benefits sorted, go to job interviews with them. They'd come out with no money and so end up thinking they had to reoffend to feed themselves. Or, they were put miles away from their families with no support. It's set up for them to fail and so I did what I could to help them fight that. I thought back to RoSA (Rape or Sexual Abuse Support Services) and wondered if I could do something to help there.

At the same time, I also applied for my Social Services records to help me remember my past. I wanted to try and face it and help myself, while trying to help others. It took a while but they sent them out without an issue, which often doesn't happen. I wasn't prepared for what I read: it was a bombshell. It made me cry, it made me angry. I couldn't believe what I was reading. It cemented everything I could remember: all there in black and white, it was an absolute disgrace.

21

'WE KNOW WHO HE IS'

The biggest shock was Terry. I was appalled we had been left so often by my mum, but the fact he was known to my mum and they let him live with us, you can't make excuses for that. She knew. To see the Social Services letter that talked more about bills than it did about me was shocking. They would say they saw him there but if she didn't fix her finances, they would pull out of any involvement – that was their focus. They sent letters and she ignored them, so they did nothing about it. There was so much detail about the financial side of our lives but they skimmed over the fact that a sex offender, who was also a killer, was living with a child. He stabbed someone over 40 times but, sure, let's concentrate on the electricity. The anger I felt reading that fuelled me and I wanted to do something about it.

In 2014, I got in touch with a lawyer in Manchester, who agreed that it was all there in black and white – that there was confirmation that Social Services had seen Terry Price at our home and still proceeded to take 'no further action' (NFA) with the case, due to Mum not co-operating over her finances. He also noted that the Probation Services had contacted Aston Social Services in 1980 and 1982 to inform them there was a convicted paedophile living at the address with two young children and nothing was done about it.

The reports were sent off to a former social worker and I was told that one of the best psychologists would do an assessment on me. Everything kept getting pushed back as the system was flooded after the Jimmy Savile debacle at the time, but finally the report was done. It was disgusting. This was the report commissioned by my solicitor, undertaken by an independent social worker, which said there was no clear evidence that there were any long-lasting effects of the abuse. I wrote to my solicitor after this, telling him how appalled I was with the report and that I doubted she had grasped what she was reading.

All I wanted was an acknowledgement of the lifetime impact my abuse and the failings around it had on me, for those in charge of my care to put their hands up and apologise and take responsibility for their failings. I was advised that I would need to take out a civil case against Birmingham City Council if I wanted any acknowledgement of any failings.

At the same time, I was doing a ten-week training course with RoSA. Through this, I started learning so much more about dissociation and more detail about PTSD. It was like a light bulb going on. You start learning about yourself – bloody hell, I'd been living with all of this and I didn't even know what half of it was called! It was like the abuse, when I didn't have the words for what was being done to me. It was a whole new world with my vocabulary opening up. There was a warning, however: when you do the course that you can become retraumatised and I was definitely affected. When I finished the course and started having clients, I was at Level 3, a counselling support worker, and I enrolled on a college course on counselling too, which would take me to Level 4 after two years, when I'd be a qualified counsellor. I had no tools at that point, and that did concern me – a point I raised. I had to teach myself a lot of it.

At first, I didn't realise that I was being retraumatised. I felt empowered, actually, and decided once again to go to the police.

I could do this.

* * *

I got in touch with North Warwickshire Police again in 2015 – I wanted to do it on my own doorstep, even though they would have to pass it on. When I was going to the police station, I could feel my body trying to close down. This time they made an appointment for me to go in and chat to a woman. She listened and took notes: 'We need to do an ABE procedure,' she said, 'that's "Achieving Best Evidence." You need to come back and we'll go into more depth.'

I didn't realise that my whole world would open up with the ABE. It was a Pandora's box. My protective bubble was gone and it was all-consuming. The sheer quantity of what I had to tell her hit me after the short first interview. I knew that I had to go back and do a video of my evidence and, in between, I realised the enormity of what I had to talk about. I had no control over the flashbacks I was experiencing, but now I had to purposely go back and tell the details. There was also the fear that I'd miss something out. I knew in my head what I wanted to get out in the first interview – all three hours of it – which was all about Terry Price.

During the first video interview, the officer was so good – she was really careful with me. It took place in a nicer setting, like a living room, and they made sure I was settled and allowed me to talk through it all at my own pace. I was given breaks when I was upset and she was attentive throughout.

At the end, she said, 'Della, this is so important. I'm going to get all of this typed up today. I'm going to drive to Birmingham and hand it to them in person.' I just felt, *wow. This is important.* She was the first person to validate my abuse; she was telling me this mattered. *This is going somewhere*, I thought.

It doesn't work like that.

When the report was passed to West Midlands Police, it took a long time for someone to contact me, going on two months, rather than the instant response I had hoped for due to the severity of what I'd been through. I had to contact them – which is how it's been through the whole process.

It was during one such phone call when a detective constable from West Midlands Police told me, 'We know who your abuser is.'

'You what?'

'We know who he is, but his name isn't Terry Price anymore.'

'What is it? What's his name now?' I expected it to be something similar – Terry something.

'It's Robert McEwan. That's what he's living under.'

So Terry really had tried to hide completely. I was in shock.

'Why has he changed his name? Has he committed more offences?' I wanted to know.

'I can't tell you that, I'm afraid.'

I didn't even know that changing your name was a thing offenders could do. Had he changed his name to evade justice? I knew from my records that he was already a sex offender when he came to live with us at 17. He had been questioned about other crimes then, he'd been convicted of manslaughter for God's sake. It was Terry Price who had committed those offences. But now, there was no Terry Price? I couldn't get my head around it. He was Robert McEwan now – what had he done in between?

My heart sank as the next question formed in my mind: 'Has he been allowed to have a family?'

'I'm sorry, I just can't give out that information.'

'So, why tell me anything? Why open the door a little and then slam it back in my face?'

All she said was, 'I'm sorry, Della.' I thought back to the time I'd spent online, before I gave my first interview, searching Friends Reunited, searching social media, trying to find Terry Price. No wonder I hadn't been able to find him; he'd got rid of all traces of that identity and was someone else in name.

'All I can say, which will hopefully be of some comfort, is that he is actually in prison at this time. We know where he is. He can't commit any further offences while he's there. The issue we have is that he plays the mental health card. He keeps managing to get transferred between the mental health unit and the main prison.'

He was in prison? Dear God, he had done something else and he was still running rings around everyone. He might not be doing anything right now while he was locked up, but what had he done to get there, what other lives had he ruined? And he was playing the system by the sounds of it. No change there then. As soon as he knew he was being questioned again about offences, he played the not-fit-to-plead card. He'd been in and out of the system, he knew the loopholes and what he could get away with.

'He's in for abusing one of his own children,' she told me eventually. 'But he's up for parole. What's happened now is that if he doesn't take responsibility for these new charges you've brought, he won't be paroled. We're in quite a good position. He has to either take responsibility or deny it and get no parole for that. He can't be released either way.' At first, I was just glad that he was in a Catch 22 position. However, he then went down the 'not fit to plead' route, saying that his health had deteriorated. I felt so let down by the system and didn't even know now whether he would even be charged.

22

THE TRIAL

I went to the police in 2015, but Terry wasn't charged until 2017. During that time, from going into that police station and him being charged, my whole life fell apart. My PTSD went through the roof, I couldn't sleep and I had so much anger that I couldn't believe I was the same person I'd been before. I had an absolute rage within me and had to hit my fists off the table all the time, as if there was sheer energy pushing through me. I couldn't process anything if there was noise, I couldn't even stand to have my grandchildren around me. Everything seemed so intense, everything from my carefully packed away box was on the surface now. My flashbacks and nightmares had all been ramped up to 100.

In 2016, the police interviewed Terry Price (as I will always call him), but it wasn't for long – he quickly played the mental health card, was put into the mental health unit and they were denied permission to interview him further. He knew the system, I didn't. He had access to all the mental health support on offer, I didn't. I continued with my counselling support role, plus college, until early 2016. The flashbacks were horrendous, I wasn't able to sleep and my physical and mental health was in decline. He didn't even have to think about life – I was a mother, I had a family, I had a house to keep up, do uniforms, get my kids to school, all the mundane things that take up a life – but he was exempt from all of that.

I was constantly fighting my body too, as it wanted to close down again. Every time the phone went, I thought it would be a call to tell me he was being charged. I don't think the police do it on purpose, but they can't imagine the horror of it, the waiting and not knowing. In 2016, they phoned me on my birthday to give me a procedural update, not even anything important. I had to compartmentalise everything, get through Christmas, get through summer, but this time I had no control. My trauma had a firm grip on me but I could only wait for other people to make decisions. My body was telling me enough was enough. I had pain every time I sat down. If I fell asleep watching telly, the kids would think I was having a fit because I would be screaming and in such a state. Ellie used to wake me up and I'd feel so guilty that I was putting her through this, making her witness it. I couldn't go into detail of what was going on, what the flashbacks were of, so I just said that I'd always had blackouts and it was nothing to worry about. I was masking it, smoothing it all over, all the while knowing I had no control over my thoughts or my body.

I'd started by thinking I could cope, but I couldn't.

Six months down the line, I had to call the police: 'I feel like I'm going mad here, I need someone to talk to.'

They put me in touch with an ISVA, an Independent Sexual Violence Advisor, and still nothing was happening with Terry.

It was January 2017, after a meeting with the Crown Prosecution Service (CPS), when they finally decided they could charge Terry Price. There was no warning that it was going to happen. I was at the hospital having some tests done when the detective constable called me.

'Good news, Della! We've got some charges – let me read it out to you.'

I was in a public place, a hospital corridor, as she reeled off the charges. I couldn't say 'not right now' because it had taken so long to get there. I'd waited so long for that moment but took in very little. Thankfully, she did email it to me afterwards and that was a huge milestone, to actually get those six charges.

Now all I had to do was wait.

* * *

A couple of weeks later, it arrived. The envelope which landed on my doormat was innocuous, the paper inside folded into three parts, the heading 'Criminal Justice System' so stark – it was all very matter of fact, there was no grand fanfare to announce just what a huge matter this was. The letter inside was dated a few days earlier and came from the Witness Care Unit. It was all laid out in a horrifying list:

Dear Mrs Wright,

Case against Mister Mac (formerly known as both Robert McEwan and Terry Price)
NOTICE TO ATTEND BIRMINGHAM CROWN COURT

I am writing to confirm that you are required to attend court to give your evidence.
Mister Mac (formerly known as Robert McEwan and Terry Price) appeared before Birmingham Crown Court on 19 April 2017 charged with the below offences:

Incite a girl under 14 years of age to commit an act of gross indecency
Gross indecency with a girl under 14 years of age
Indecent assault on a girl under 16 years of age
Indecent assault on a girl under 14 years of age
(x 2 charges)

He has still not entered a plea to these charges and another plea hearing will take place on 15 June 2017 at Birmingham Crown Court. However, in anticipation of a not guilty plea, the court has set a trial date. If the defendant pleads guilty at the hearing on 15 June 2017 then the trial will not go ahead and the defendant will be sentenced. If the defendant pleads not guilty then the trial will go ahead. The defendant is still in custody. The trial, should it go ahead, is set to begin on 11 September 2017 at Birmingham Crown Court. It is expected to last for 4 days.

There was a warning that dates or times could change and that there was someone to talk to if I was worried, but all I could think was, *he'll say he isn't guilty – he won't want to miss out on the show, on putting me through it.*

I couldn't have counselling while I waited – it's not recommended by the police as it can be used against you. You get that far, you won't let anything be used against you – it feels like you're the one on trial. I also knew that it was frowned upon that I was working with RoSa. I knew that his barristers could request any counselling notes and that these could be used against me.

I had to hold onto the fact that he was deemed fit to plead. He was brought before the Magistrates' Court in March 2017, but it isn't really explained that it doesn't mean much, it's just part of the process so that it proceeds to Crown Court. It's ticking a box. It was just a plea hearing but there was no phone call to let me know what had happened. Victim Support called the next day to tell me it hadn't even gone ahead because of delays and admin.

'I haven't been able to sleep, I haven't been able to breathe,' I told them.

'Oh, it's not important – this is just what goes on. It doesn't matter if he pleads guilty or not, it'll have to go to Crown Court anyway. You'll get another date.'

The new date was another month of waiting and I didn't want to get worked up, but I couldn't help it. I was used to being let down. At 5pm that day, I got a call:

'It did go ahead today but he wasn't able to enter a plea.'

'Why on earth not?'

'He's changed his name again.'

'To what? What is it this time?'

'He's now called Mister Mac.'

'What the hell?! He's in prison, how can he do that?'

'He's perfectly entitled – but he wants to be addressed by that name and that name alone. We can't put the charges to him because they're not in his name anymore.'

I collapsed on the floor, still holding the phone, screaming, 'I can't do this, I can't do this any longer. What does this mean? Can he not be charged now?' It was a joke, it made a mockery of everything. He sounded like some sort of children's entertainer.

'I'll get the police to call you.'

They did call a few days later, telling me that they could go ahead but they'd have to start from scratch with the paperwork, making sure it was all in this new name that he'd made up for himself.

'We know what he's doing. We've set a Crown Court date before he's even pleaded as he's just playing a game at this point. It'll be September.'

He had to go back and plead again in his new name – he pleaded not guilty, which was what we had expected. For my own sanity, there were times when I thought I couldn't carry on and I would probably have given up without the IVSA. I knew you could have screens in the court, but no one actually offered them to me and I had to ask for them. I didn't want to know what he looked like or for him to see me; I was prepared that he would be there, but I couldn't take actually seeing him. There was a trip to the court to give me an idea of what I would be walking into and my dad came with me. He was very supportive by that point – naturally, Mum wasn't. She was going to be called as a witness but I wanted nothing to do with it. You could see real guilt on Dad's face and he was incredibly apologetic: 'I did try to get custody of you, Della, but I had no chance because of my criminal convictions.'

'I know, Dad, I know.'

He was there constantly from that point: 'I'm always on the end of the phone for you and I'll be here whenever you need me. I haven't been in the past, but that all changes now. You mean the world to me and I just want to show you how much I love you, even though I know I've failed you in the past.'

I wasn't sceptical – I actually felt very protective of him. I knew he was trying to make up for the past and I didn't want to burden him with how bad things had been, I didn't want him to have those pictures in his head.

I was terrified of crossing paths with Terry. I'd heard horror stories of that happening. You only meet your barrister on the morning of the trial, they just read it all off the paperwork, it's another case on the list to them. My barrister was really nice and friendly although he immediately told me something I wasn't prepared for.

'Terry isn't actually going to appear today.'

'What do you mean? Special treatment again?'

'They actually feel that he is such a dangerous offender, they have nowhere to safely hold him – there aren't the facilities here.'

'How dare they?! How dare HE! I'm here, I'm ready, but he's getting off with things again?'

'We've come this far, Della – we need to get this done before he starts playing the mental health card again. It's not ideal but this is still an opportunity. We need to proceed.'

I didn't have a choice anyway.

'Well, if he's not here, I don't need a screen. I'll just go in there.'

For the whole first day of the trial on 11th September 2017, I knew I was going first as I was the one who had reported it, but that would be after the 'admin' of swearing in the jury and things like that. It was getting towards half past four, when I knew the Court would close down for the day, that I was told: 'We're not going to go in today,' my barrister said.

I started to relax a little. I'd get home to my own house, my own bed tonight, and gear myself up for tomorrow. He'd no sooner said that when I was called.

Why call me now, why not leave me in peace until tomorrow? I asked myself.

I had to go in.

It was the most nerve-wracking experience of my life. The jury and judge were there – and the big screen, like a huge TV, with him on it. I wasn't prepared; I felt sick. *God, now I know what he looks like and I never wanted that.* I had been ten years old the last time I'd seen that face.

He was wearing the most ridiculous wig, a big, black curly thing that was laughable. I felt as if he was stamping on me, as if he was making sure I knew that I was nothing in all of this. He looked like Coco the Clown. The whole way he was able to have power throughout was disgusting; they were now allowing him into court, an official place, letting him sit there like that. I knew what else he was doing – he was trying to disguise himself so that I wouldn't recognise him and it would all fall apart.

It was a livestream: I could see all of his reactions and he could see me, he could see everything. I had said I didn't need a screen because I'd been told he wouldn't be there, but he was: he was there.

Straight away, his barrister was up. I'd been briefed it was their job to undermine me, to make me slip up. I needed to stick to the facts and not get into anything confrontational. I knew what was true, if I didn't understand or remember then I needed to say that. Immediately, she said that I'd got him mixed up with his brother.

'I don't even know his brother – I've never met him,' I replied.

She couldn't go down that road so she tried another: 'I believe you are confusing the defendant with your stepfather, Aaron.'

This was ludicrous.

'How in the world could I get them mixed up? Aaron is a black Nigerian and Terry Price is white and Scottish.'

The jury even laughed at that point.

'Mister Mac,' she corrected me.

I would never call him that. I would never let him dictate to me in that way and to have me refer to him by that ridiculous name.

Terry Price – because that's his name – was rude and obnoxious throughout. I could hear him huffing and puffing throughout my evidence. On the occasions I did look over at the screen, he was rolling his eyes at what I was saying. That was about all that happened on the first day before we were adjourned. I was shaking when we left, knowing that I'd been attacked from the moment I got there, and I was heading home with his face in my head. I was due to be on the stand first thing the next morning and knew what was coming.

The police told me they knew Terry's barrister would take that approach but they didn't want to forewarn me as I needed to answer things naturally.

'You did really well, just keep going the way you did then and it'll be OK,' the detective told me.

I could see their point but the whole experience, even though it was only 30 minutes, had left me shaken.

'And that wig!' I exclaimed. 'How in the world did he even get that in prison? Had he been allowed to make an official request for what was effectively a clown wig, which had then been processed as completely fine, then he was given it to wear remotely in court? No one saw any problem with that?'

She looked carefully at her colleague, then back to me. 'Della, when I went to interview him in prison, he was wearing a cowboy hat,' she told me.

'Has he got a props department in there?' I would have laughed if it hadn't been such a kick in the teeth. Maybe he was just acting mad, playing the mental health card again?

23

NOWHERE TO HIDE

I had a horrendous night then was called straight in the next day, although only for an hour or so. Terry Price didn't have his wig on any longer, just his own short, dark hair. Once I gave my evidence, I was allowed to go into the public gallery to sit with my dad. He squeezed my hand throughout everything. Then it was time for Mum. She staggered in, limping with a walking stick. *Poor me*. She didn't even glance in my direction. All I'd been told was that, when the police interviewed her, she'd said in her statement that I had encouraged him.

At six years old?

How could a mother say that? How could she say a child of that age had, basically, asked for rape and sexual abuse?

In court, they asked her about her relationship with Terry.

'It was his brother I had a relationship with,' she claimed.

I didn't remember that at all, it was news to me. All I could think was that, when Terry was moved to the hostel and she slept with a man in the bed next to me, that was maybe his brother. She claimed that she only met Terry through this brother but I knew that wasn't true, as the time she'd slept with him next to me was after Terry had moved out. She was doing anything she could to absolve herself of responsibility.

After Mum was done, there was a point where Terry's character references were heard. His previous convictions couldn't be brought in as they would influence the jury, but these character references did him no favours either.

Towards the end of that day, Terry was interviewed a little and was incredibly rude to his own barrister. I can't even remember the questions, just how awful he was, even getting up and walking away at some point.

On the third day, I was completely exhausted. To be honest, once you've given your evidence, the court isn't interested in you anyway: you've done your bit. I didn't attend that day as Terry was giving his evidence and I didn't want to hear it – I knew it would all be lies anyway. Not being there was excruciating and much worse than I'd anticipated. Not knowing what was going on, not getting updates, so I decided to go back on the fourth day for the summing up and the jury being sent out. However, on that third day, one of the points raised was the fact that Terry was in prison for the abuse of another little girl. Apparently, he was extremely angry about that and said he had only been showing affection to her and nothing more. I knew what Terry's 'affection' was like.

'They got it wrong,' he'd said. Then, incredibly, he added, 'but there are another four that haven't come forward, have they?'

My barrister said that it was as if Terry knew he was losing, so he just didn't care. He was trying to take any sliver of control back by throwing it in their faces that he knew more than them and that they had no idea of the extent of what he had done.

I was in the Public Gallery again with Dad the next day while the judge gave every detail of every charge. Dad had never heard those details. It was brutal. All we could do was hug each other, but you are told not to be over-emotional in case the jury is swayed and you have to keep things under wraps to a large extent. The jury was sent out to consider their verdict.

'What happens now?' I asked my barrister.

'You have to stay here.'

'But it could be hours, it could be days before they come back.'

'You're right, but you have to stay on the premises – if you go out, no one will be able to let you know when the jury comes back.'

It was only because there were some trainee solicitors sitting in, watching the trial, that allowed for one of them to help. One of them said they'd WhatsApp me to let me know if anything happened and I was incredibly grateful.

We'd only just got up the road for lunch and ordered when I got the message:

They're coming back.

We were 20 minutes away and had to run all the way back – we wouldn't have made it if my barrister hadn't gone missing deliberately. We all got back into court and there were six charges. Each one was read out:

Guilty.

Guilty.

Guilty.

Guilty.

Guilty.

Guilty.

One after another.

All of them.

To hear that was just amazing.

***

I feel that it is vitally important to include my Victim
Impact Statement in full here as it is one of the things
that can really prey on the minds of anyone asked to
go down the route of pressing charges. You worry that
you'll forget something, that you will get it muddled
up or that the person reading it won't care. You think
they won't like you and that is more important than
anything. You fear that your throat will close up or
your tongue will get too big for your mouth as you
tell yourself your own story, that your fingers won't
be able to hold the pen or type the letters. You are
terrified of being silenced all over again.

This is what I said:

'I have been asked by DC [name] of West Midlands
Police to provide a witness impact statement with
regards to the sexual abuse I suffered as a child,
by Terry Price. I am finding writing this very
difficult and have continually put it off because
it has such a huge negative effect on my physical
and mental health, which I am currently trying to
manage with medication and assistance from a
mental health team and my GP.

'I was a vulnerable child who was easy prey
for Terry. My mother had mental health issues

and had recently separated from my father, who had started a new relationship. Being starved of affection and already subject to neglect, I initially welcomed the attention that he gave me. He would tell me that I was a princess and very special. He knew that I loved Elvis Presley and would promise to buy me a singing Elvis doll from the local shopping centre – it was the iconic doll of him in his white diamante suit. He would take us out on trips to his probation office and we'd visit the pet shop on the way home, where they had a parrot that talked. I'd never seen anything like that before. He would give me his undivided attention when I danced and sang to *Top of the Pops*. My mum was making me a royal blue swinging Teddy Girl skirt and he would get me to put this on and dance for him. Those dances soon turned into stripping. I had no idea that this was wrong and lapped up the attention.

'When the sexual abuse started, again I had no idea what this was – he made it appear normal, thought I did not like it. He would promise to buy me things if I kept quiet. I would scream when my mum went out at night and left us in his care because I knew what would happen when she went. But I was too young to verbalise what it was. He thrust me into an adult world that I had no words for and so I was just seen as a naughty, uncontrollable child who my mother couldn't wait to have a break from.

'I was a lonely child at school who found it difficult to make friends. I was often bullied and ostracised by my peers because I was different. At school, I would often run away and have to be chased by the "wag woman" whilst taking off my clothes and throwing them so that she would slow down to pick them up. I would want to get home to my mum because I knew that while I was with her, I was safe and when she wasn't there, bad things happened. I feel that no one, not the school or my mother, ever tried to understand what was happening for me, instead they just thought this was more proof I was a problem child.

'My mother found my pants down the back of the sofa on one occasion and I was told off for leaving them there. I found this very confusing as I hadn't left them, Terry had. So, when I had faeces in my knickers after being abused, I would wash them in the sink so that I didn't get into trouble again. This became a regular occurrence.

'I have difficulty with my adult relationships because I find that partners will either not understand me and my trauma, or if I am able to open up to them, they then use my past as a weapon against me. I also find it hard to trust people and allow anyone to get too close for fear they will see that I am broken, damaged goods or they will abuse me too.

'I am currently under the care of the Mental Health team, I have ongoing mental health issues such as PTSD, Moderate Depressions and Lack or Loss of Sexual Desire. I am prescribed the anti-depressant Sertraline and hypnotic agent Zopiclone for my insomnia. I also have Chronic Fatigue Syndrome and IBS, which is monitored by my GP.

'Since reporting to the police in 2015, my physical and mental health issues have been exacerbated, to the point that I have felt that I do not want to be here any longer. Though after taking an overdose in 2001, I know that is not an option I would ever want to take again, as I have children who need me and so I have learned to open up and request help from the appropriate services.

'Naively I thought that once I had reported, things would move swiftly, he would be charged and it would all finally be over. But this has not been the case. We are now two years down the line and I have at times wished that I never told the police. The personal cost has been huge with regards to my physical and mental health. I have lost my partner of four years, I had to quit my role as a counselling support worker with a charity that supports abuse survivors, I had to leave my CPCAB counselling course, I no longer socialise with friends and have become isolated, my children have suffered because I am no longer able to take them to after-school activities, my youngest son had to leave his football team and I am unable to look after my own grandchildren because the responsibility of keeping anyone else's children safe is too huge to bear.

'Now that he has been charged, I feel there is finally an end in sight. I appreciate that it is absolutely out of my hands and that it is up to the CPS, Courts, and a Jury to decide how this concludes. I have done everything in my power to gain justice for what Terry Price did to me, for the life I was robbed of at an early age. I can never change that, I will never know how my life could have been if he had never been in it. I will most likely continue to recall the abuse for the rest of my life. Though I hope that with psychotherapy this may be alleviated, I will never have the career I could have had if I had not had PTSD in varying degrees since the abuse in my early infancy. I will never know what it means to have an intimate relationship that doesn't cause physical pain. I will never know what it truly feels like to be vulnerable and have trust in people.

'A cliché that gets bandied around is that child sexual abuse survivors have been given a life sentence. I can testify that, at 43, this is true. Terry Price gave me a life sentence and I didn't deserve it at any point.

'I had hoped that Terry would have grown some sort of conscience in his adult life and taken responsibility for the harm he has caused me, but no, instead he is denying it and pleading not guilty, meaning that I now have to endure a trial too. It is the final insult and I hope he has to pay dearly as a result.

'It is my hope that this man never gets released from prison, so that he is never able to harm an innocent child again. If my standing up and speaking out makes this a possibility, then it has been worth the turmoil and I would gladly do it again.'

* * *

I had been through so much to get there and that one word, GUILTY, was amazing. It was a win, a victory of some kind, but do you celebrate something like that? I was exhausted from it. Dad and the kids were all at mine that weekend and I fell straight back into drinking that night. I was sick then fell asleep in the hot tub, having to be dragged out. It was a release but it was the beginning of me drinking myself into oblivion again to escape things.

The sentence wasn't immediate because they had to cross-reference old laws from when the offences took place. My barrister wanted the maximum sentence but that all took time, two months in the end. The sentencing was set for the afternoon, all of my anxiety was back. My whole body shook, I felt like I was trembling from the inside out, from my skeleton to my skin. I had to hold my breath, clench my fists and jaw, just to try and stop the shaking. My whole body was in agony. I couldn't' sit still and was pacing the room, desperately wanting to run so far away but knowing I had to stay – but we were at the end of the road. However, the morning trial at the court ran over and the sentencing was delayed until a couple of weeks later. At that point, I thought it would happen again, that I'd be waiting a lifetime for justice, as it had been the pattern all the way through.

Thankfully, it didn't and that day was one of the moments when I genuinely thought, *there's justice now, at least a bit.* It had crossed my mind that he would get away with it in the darkest way possible – by killing himself. If he'd done that, it would have left me with everything and he would have the last laugh. He was on the screen again, but not in any of his weird get-ups. The judge had to tell him to sit down and listen as Terry was being so rude. When the sentencing was read out, he flipped his chair back and stormed off. He got 22 years. He's in the mental health unit again but that won't get him out – he'll have his sentence reduced by a third like so many of them do, but then he'll be released on licence for five years.

Soon there was a letter to confirm it all, again from the Witness Care Unit – as if I would forget: *At the hearing on 24 November 2017 at Birmingham Crown Court, Mister Mac was sentenced. He was found guilty at trial of sexual offences involving children.* I wrote it down on a piece of paper, for me, each word making it seem more real as the sheet of lined A4 filled up, more real than the official letter in some ways:

Three charges of indecently assaulting Della
(counts 3, 4 and 5)
Counts 7 and 9
Count 1
Counts 2 and 6.

The total sentence was 22 years' imprisonment and five years on extended licence. His earliest release date was to be in 12 and a half years, but that would be subject to the parole board deciding if he should ever be allowed out at all, never mind before the 27 years were up.

There was a power to writing it all down, to seeing it there in black and white and knowing that I had done that. I had made sure that people knew what he had done, that it was all stacked up and no one could deny it now.

You think that once you go through the process you'll feel strong, empowered, victorious. That didn't happen for me. Instead I was left feeling retraumatised and used. I was spat out by the justice system once it was all over. I'd laid myself raw to put this man away and now I was left with the consequences. I was wide open, where would I go now? I had concentrated on this for such a long time and now I was faced with it being behind me in legal terms, but still with me in every moment of my real life.

I was seeing a mental health social worker once a week during the court process, but that was only to prop me up for the case. I was put on a waiting list for EMDR, the process of eye movement desensitisation and reprogramming, which takes the individual back to the point of their trauma, briefly and safely. You then face the images, emotions, thoughts and everything else connected with that trauma before the brain goes through reprocessing to recover. It's psychotherapy, but hugely more effective than other approaches. I wasn't allowed it while going through court, at which point there was still a nine-month waiting list in front of me.

I didn't know how to live with it. I could barely leave the house, but that social worker went above and beyond. She came to my house for sessions and encouraged me to work through my dissociation. I was sent on a course but there were ten people in the room, all with different issues, and it was miles away from what I needed. The woman running the courses did EMDR and acknowledged that was what I needed. When she went off sick, there was no one at all in the whole area that did that process so I was offered CBT again.

In March 2017, my solicitor raised a claim to the High Court of Justice stating that Birmingham City Council had known everything. They knew that I had been subject to Supervision Orders and Place of Safety Orders, that I had been referred to Social Services and that social work intervention had been ineffective in the past: 'It would take too long to describe the number of complaints received.' Mum had been described as 'an immature, manipulative liar,' who did not keep to agreements. They knew that by the time Terry Price was living with Mum that he was on a care order for indecency and attempted rape as well as having already been convicted of a sexual offence against a 12-year-old girl, but it took two years for a probation officer to raise concerns about him being there. He never did get moved to the bail hostel that was planned for him.

My lawyer emphasised the key term *duty of care*. We knew that it had never been adhered to, that I had never been protected from *foreseeable risks of harm*, or from *ill treatment and neglect*, but would they accept their failings? There was such a list of what they had got wrong, it seemed unlikely they could escape from the truth of how they had let me down. Their duty of care should have encompassed:

A duty to protect [me] from foreseeable risks of harm.

A duty to protect [me] from ill-treatment and neglect.

A duty to provide a range and level of services as appropriate to [me].

A duty to safeguard and promote [my] development in a manner appropriate to [my] stage of development at any given time.

A duty at all times to provide a competent and suitably qualified and experienced social worker or workers whose responsibility it was to monitor the physical and psychological welfare of [me].

A duty to protect [me] from neglect, physical, emotional, and psychological damage.

A duty to report any abuse or neglect that [I] was known or thought likely to have suffered.

A duty to ensure that [I] received appropriate treatment for any injury (including a psychiatric injury) that [I] was known or thought likely to have suffered.

A duty to monitor [my] physical, emotional, psychiatric and psychological welfare.

A duty to visit and speak to [me] and ascertain her views, wishes, anxieties and complaints in as far as was appropriate to [my] age, disabilities and understanding.

A duty to ascertain whether [she] was placed in immediate danger or at risk of harm from any of the adults with whom she was living or having contact with or could be placed at risk of harm by them.

A duty to act appropriately and sufficiently to keep [me] safe from harm, which the available information indicated that [she] was or may be suffering or was at risk of suffering.

It was a lot of words to say one thing – *you didn't keep this little girl safe.*

* * *

After the trial ended, the three-year battle I'd had with the civil case against Birmingham City Council collapsed. A court ruling on a case called CN vs Poole[1] ruled that Social Services could not be held responsible for children not physically in their care, that is, not formally in a children's home or in foster care. This ruling would have devastating consequences for many victims and survivors who had been let down by their local authorities. My solicitor advised the only route I had left was to apply to the Criminal Injuries Compensation scheme, however he noted they were notoriously difficult. The battle with them was like nothing I could have envisaged. The trial might have ended in 2017, but what they put me through was appalling and it didn't end for another three years.

I had to keep telling my story to so many people, keep going over it, with social workers, lawyers, psychiatrists, psychologists, recounting every last detail of the abuse time after time. It's inhumane. If I'd known at the start what it involved, I would never have started. But I still had another battle to fight. When I had approached a solicitor in 2015 to look into the lack of protection I had been given as a child, they

---

1 http://insurance.dwf.co.uk/news-updates/2019/06/cn-v-poole-borough-council-unanimous-supreme-court-decision-changes-the-landscape-for-failure-to-remove-claims

had instructed an Independent Social Work Consultant to look over my files in order that she could give her opinion as to whether I had a claim against the Social Work Department. It had shocked me at the time, the fact that she could see so little of how things had really affected me.

Her report had contained this: 'I have now had the opportunity to review the papers in this matter, many of which are redacted and some of which are illegible. It is also the case that there appear to be no records for some periods pertinent to the potential claim [...]

'(The claimant) clearly suffered from neglect and sustained a number of injuries during their early infancy.' The consultant pointed out that the files recorded I had been left unattended in the family home in 1975 as well as evidence of parental neglect, including Mum frequently leaving me unattended and neglecting any of my medical needs. Despite this, there 'were no concerns for [Della's] welfare ... there continued to be many referrals, six between December 1975 and October 1976,' during which time they knew I was being left unattended in the house again. That was when a Place of Safety Order was obtained for a month, the one which Mum agreed to voluntarily. There are records which agree I briefly returned home and was then readmitted to care between January and November 1977 as she was in hospital again with mental health issues but those records pretty much stop between then and 1978 when my case was closed.

The report continued: 'It is noted in late 1977 that the father had been in prison and one reference suggests that past neglect [...] in part reflected marital tensions. There was no further involvement for two years. Between April 1980 and April 1982, the mother appears to have been cohabiting with a schedule one offender. There is no evidence that any risk assessment or protective action was taken.'

That was it, until 1988, '... it was learnt that Della had been pregnant the previous March and that she had an abusive partner. Given that she was not yet sixteen years old at that time it does seem odd that no one seems to have enquired further about this.'

Despite all of this, the consultant still didn't believe it was enough: 'To summarise, there is little evidence that [Della's] development or health was being impaired as a result of the care provided to them to a level that would have satisfied a court that she should have been permanently removed from the mother's care prior to 1980. It is also not clear to me what harm [Della] reportedly suffered as a result of any alleged negligence on the part of the defendant.'

I'd felt so let down when I read all of that. Taking each point made, I noted in a letter to my lawyer that while there was a lot of material missing or redacted in the files, there was still enough in there to show that I had been failed by the system. They conceded that no risk assessment or protective action had been undertaken when Mum admitted Terry Price into our home, knowing that he was a convicted sexual offender. It was clear that rather than take the family history into account as a whole – neglect, injuries sustained, Mum's long-term mental health issues and her appalling judgement around who she let into my life – that the Social Services team took each referral as a single, isolated incident. Their failing to understand the complex history of the life I lived most certainly did have a huge and long-lasting impact on my health and development. There were so many people who had witnessed things back then and if only they had put them together and seen the whole picture, perhaps the outcome might have been different, perhaps I could have been saved before Terry Price even came into the equation.

I told the lawyer – again – of those times when I'd had to be dragged to school, of taking my clothes and shoes off on the way, of the many visits to our house of the 'wag' woman, going on into secondary school, where I became sexually active far too young. Why did no one ask questions about a 14-year-old being pregnant, or offer any guidance when it ended so badly? Why did no one ask questions when I was pregnant again at 15? When I was moved to the school for pregnant schoolgirls, was there really no liaison between social work and department of education? Why wasn't I flagged as vulnerable? Did I suffer? Of course I did. Mentally, educationally, emotionally, I was less than I could have been and no one stepped in to say *this isn't right*.

It made me incredibly angry that the consultant's report said that 'it is not clear to me what harm [Della] reportedly suffered as a result of any alleged negligence on the part of the [authorities].' It wasn't alleged – it was my life.

In 2016, there was another report, this time by a psychiatrist. Again, this was commissioned by my solicitor in preparation for the civil case against Birmingham City Council (which was ended by the CN vs Poole case ruling in 2017, which is why I had to lodge a case with the Criminal Injuries Compensation Authority/CICA).

'Ms Wright tells me that Terrence [Price] started living with them when she was six years old until he was sent to prison and on being released from prison came back to live with them. She recollects him being in contact with them until she was 11 years old. Ms Wright tells me that Terrence would get her to dance for him and strip her clothes. She states that she did not know that this was wrong and felt happy to get some attention. She told me that he would also make her masturbate him orally and they would both be naked on her mother's bed with him on top of her … they had penetrative sex vaginally and anally as she recollects washing her pants, which had faecal matter in them. Ms Wright tells me that this abuse would occur 3–4 times a week whenever her mother went out. She recollects screaming and begging her mother not to leave her alone with Terrance (sic). She states that she did not understand what was happening and was unable to verbalise it.

'Ms Wright feels that she would dissociate during these incidences and therefore cannot totally recall what would happen. She states that on one occasion it was her Nan's funeral and her mother did not take her with her and Terrance (sic) sexually abused her. She recollects being physically unwell after this and not being able to eat for a few days.

'Ms Wright tells me that she was in a one-year relationship at the age of 13 with her partner and fell pregnant at the age of 14 years. He was 5–6 years older to (sic) her. She tells me that this was an ectopic pregnancy that had to be terminated. She feels that she did not fully understand her ectopic pregnancy and though her mother was initially supportive, she felt lonely and isolated.

'Ms Wright tells me that her partner was physically

abusive to her and her mother had to get an injunction to stop him from coming to the house. Ms Wright tells me that she does not know why questions were not asked about this inappropriate relationship considering her young age.

'Ms Wright tells me that at the age of 14 years she attended Cardinal Wiseman Secondary School in Kingstanding until the age of 15 years when she fell pregnant with Laura. Following this she was transferred to a pregnant girls' school in Erdington for a period of six months.'

This was all true, this was accurate, but seeing it written down so coldly still raised a million questions for me – although those questions had never been asked by anyone else. There had been so little time when the consultant had undertaken my psychiatric assessment and I felt that the ongoing effects of the abuse, especially the anxiety, really hadn't been considered properly. I wanted her to know the many, many ways in which my daily life was still affected and I asked that my letter be passed on and included in her report. It was so difficult to write it all down, to see it in black and white, because I had never really admitted – even to myself – the extent of the impact. It had always been so much simpler to say, 'I'm OK,' but this was my chance to get it all out, and if no one else cared, at least I had said the words.

Looking back at all those records, now that Terry had nowhere to hide, really brought it home to me that I had to find the strength to continue fighting the last battle – the battle to show they hadn't kept to their duty of care and that someone had to acknowledge that.

24

DUTY OF CARE

What people need to understand is that the rest of life goes on. Abuse can consume so much of you, but the world doesn't stop – and there was more waiting for me.

There's no denying my relationship with Dad was a complicated one. The best thing he had going for him was that he wasn't Mum – but that didn't make him perfect. I fully accept that in the early days of their relationship, he was violent to her, he drank, he was out a lot, he was a womaniser. He wasn't in my life a great deal when I was little, sometimes because he was in prison, sometimes because he was off with another woman, and as I got older, I realised that they were both incredibly selfish people. I wanted to hold onto the fact that Dad had tried to get custody at one point and that Mum had coached me into saying that I chose her, but the truth was, I barely knew him anyway.

When they got back together in 1991, it was initially hard to accept him in my life given what she had said about him, but I did try. From the time I was 18, we had something better. He had changed – actually, Mum had changed a bit too as she was very different as a gran. It was much more in her comfort zone – being a mother had never really been her cup of tea, to say the least. I was on my own with Laura and James, and the time I spent with Dad, building a relationship through music, was important to me. There was no doubt he had been a rogue, but age had mellowed him and he did everything by the book at that point. After Mum left us all high and dry to go to Turkey with her lottery winnings, I helped him get a flat sorted and make it a nice place. We'd phone each other for hours and I'd struggle to get away – he always had one more thing to tell me, no matter how long we chatted. He was lonely, there were no more women to be chased and he was making the effort to be there for me.

'I'm so sorry I was never there for you, Della,' he told me just before the court case. 'I'll never forgive myself for not being able to stop what that bastard did to you. All I can do is be here for you now. It's too little, too late, but it's all I have.' I did appreciate his apology – 'sorry' was all I had ever wanted from my parents.

Mum never apologised, she made everything about her – I felt Dad was genuine and the way in which he stood by me throughout the 2017 trial was testament to that. He never left my side and held my hand throughout. He just didn't seem right though. I could see he was unwell and I worried myself sick that it was because of what he was hearing in court, what he was being forced to face up to when bombarded with evidence about what I had been through. I saw a big difference when we went back in the November for the sentencing. Dad was even weaker, he had a chest infection and seemed completely worn down. He'd just had the flu vaccine at that point and I assumed it was side effects, but he never quite got over it. In the December, he called me and said that he had been prescribed antibiotics but was planning to be with us all on New Year's Day.

I got a call that morning: 'Della, love – I'm not going to make it today. I'm really sorry but I just can't travel like this. My chest feels like someone is standing on it. I'm just going to rest for the day and I'll call you tomorrow.' He never really did get over it, and when he told me in the January that he'd been advised to get the pneumonia vaccination, I was dead set against it:

'I don't think you've been right since the flu jab, Dad – are you sure you want to risk getting side effects from this one too?'

He was adamant – this might be the thing which could perk him up a bit. Two weeks later, his neighbours found him unconscious on the floor of his flat. He was rushed to hospital that day, Friday, and the doctors said he had sepsis and pneumonia. I couldn't understand that at all – he'd not long had the pneumonia jab which should surely have made catching it unlikely?

By the Sunday, there was no sign of improvement and Dad was taken to Intensive Care. It wasn't looking good and my daughter Laura, now a nurse, agreed. However, when he got to ICU, he seemed to perk up a bit and when I went in the next day, although he was on dialysis, he was eating ice cream.

'You're looking much better!' I told him.

'I'm feeling it, love, I'm feeling it,' he replied.

'What are you staring at that clock for, though?' I asked, pointing to the old-fashioned ward clock he hadn't taken his eyes off.

'I'm concentrating on getting better – every minute that passes is a minute closer to me getting out. Will you do a few things for me? Pop over to the flat and clean out the fridge, if you don't mind. I did a big batch cook before I came in here and it'll all be going off. Stick some money on the electric as well and I think it might be a good idea to talk to the housing people – I'm going to need to go into sheltered accommodation when I get out of here, get a bit of help in case I'm poorly again.'

That last request was a bit odd as he was usually so self-reliant, but I was pleased he was making plans, it felt like a good sign. I left him watching his favourite quiz show with one of the nurses and went home. Finally, I could breathe again. I'd been worried about the flu and pneumonia jabs affecting him, but my biggest concern had been whether the trial and sentencing had knocked Dad for six. If it had, I'd blame myself.

I got home, made something to eat and put *EastEnders* on the telly. Within minutes, the phone rang: it was Dad's sister.

'Della, you need to get back to the hospital, it's not good.'

Dad was suffering from internal bleeding and his whole system was shutting down. As soon as I got there, the doctors rushed me into a side room.

'We need your permission, Mrs Wright,' they said.

'For what?' I was in a daze. I knew they'd been talking but it had all washed over me.

'We need to remove your father's stomach to give him any chance.'

'God, no! He'd never want that! What sort of life would he have if you did that to him?'

'It's something I urge you to consider, as quickly as possible ...' the doctor reiterated, but before he could finish, the door opened.

'He's getting rushed to surgery now,' someone shouted at me. I couldn't honestly say who it was, everything was a blur. I ran to Dad's bed, where everyone was crowded round – his sisters, his brother, my kids. Before I knew it, they were taking Dad to the operating theatre and no one was asking my permission about anything. We were beyond choices now, they would just do anything they could to save him.

I went to get a hot drink and as I stood at the vending machine, my cheek pressed against the glass, unable to make even the simplest of choices, I saw a doctor walk towards me.

I knew what he was going to say, I just knew it.

Dad was gone. He'd had a massive heart attack on the way to theatre and taken all of the decisions out of our hands.

It was so sudden. How could he have been eating ice cream and watching a quiz show a few hours ago and now he was dead? Was this my fault? Had I brought it on through him seeing and hearing everything in court? He was only 64, no age at all really, and I blamed myself. Yet again, I cursed ever going down this route, ever telling the police what Terry Price had done to me. The anger coursed through me and I have to admit that

I thought, *why not her, why not Mum? She's no use, why take the decent parent and leave her behind?*

Over the next few days, I arranged a lovely humanist ceremony for Dad, who had been an atheist. I thought of all the times we'd managed to find together in recent years and of the music which had bound us together. I knew that he had been a devil when he was younger, but he was a good person at heart. He had mellowed a lot in his later years, he knew that I would not stand for his earlier racist views, and I truly believe I had in some ways educated him. We'd found our peace and he had the ability to admit his faults, taking responsibility for them, which was more than my mother had ever been able to do.

25

SURVIVING

I now know that so many other 'survivors' have similar feelings and reactions to me. I put 'survivors' in quotation marks there quite deliberately because, despite it being the politically correct way to describe the army of us out there, sometimes I feel that I'm not surviving at all, I'm just existing. I knew then that when other people meet me, I can seem 'normal', but that is because I have had to play down and suppress my emotions. People (family, friends, school, Social Services, police) have either brushed me off or told me that I'm a liar, attention-seeking, plain naughty, or making a scene. That takes its toll. While on the surface I may appear fine, or even specifically say that I'm fine, in my head I'm looking for an escape route, wanting to get whatever it is over with and wondering how quickly I can get to safety. Often I feel like I'm an imposter, that I don't belong, that I'll be found out or exposed. I don't like to draw attention to myself, I don't want people to look too closely at me or make judgements. To combat that, I've relied too heavily on alcohol in the past as that lowers my inhibitions, or act in an overly joking way to minimise how I feel, or put up walls and appear cold. Does that sound familiar to you? If you've been abused, I bet it does. If you haven't, you're probably exhausted reading it. Well, buckle up because I've barely started.

I'm always watching people, noting where their words and actions don't match, double speak is everywhere and I can no longer tolerate it. This has had dire consequences over the years for my personal relationships – there have been many cases where I can see, early on, that something isn't right, that there is a behaviour which raises my internal alarm, but I override that gut feeling and make excuses for them, only to become angry at myself for not acting on my intuition when it all goes to hell. There have been too many times with men where I feel I have only just awoken from a bad dream once they show their true colours and I wonder how I got to that place. It's as if the child part of me has been in charge, been taken advantage of again, then the adult part of me wakes up and thinks what the fuck has gone on here? There are times when it just seems impossible to escape from the past. I know that I get lost or lose myself in relationships, which means that I attract dominant men who want a woman like me, a woman who will allow their needs to be put first. When I do find the courage or conviction to stand up for myself, they use my past as a weapon or leave.

When partners buy me gifts or are nice to me in any way, I am triggered into flashbacks and emotional dysregulation. Terry Price used gifts to groom me and keep me quiet – to this day, I can't ask for or accept help or gifts because I feel like the price would be too high to pay, I would be indebted and who knows what they would ask for in return? I see ulterior motives everywhere.

I always seem to be ready to cut people out of my life, finding changes to agreed meetings or times disproportionately overwhelming, again triggering me to close down. I find social gatherings and events overwhelming. If I can bring myself to attend, I feel disconnected. It isn't that I don't want to be there, I do, I want to do what other people do, but because of the numbness which takes over, I just avoid going. I avoid family outings and parties because going just emphasises to me how abnormal I am.

Even when I'm at home, in my safe space, things can be bad. I have regular meltdowns where I sit on the floor picking pieces off the carpet, real and imaginary, if anyone has come to my house unannounced when I've just finished cleaning. I clean a lot when I am physically able to, I now have chronic fatigue syndrome (CFS/ME) and fibromyalgia (a long-term condition that causes pain all over the body) to add to the long list of physical and mental health issues, all trauma induced. It doesn't matter how much I like or even love people around me, I feel invaded, my privacy has been attacked and everything needs to be cleaned again from the beginning. I internalise the anger I feel about the intrusion even when they are dear to me, even when they are my own children and grandchildren. As soon as they leave, I will clean, vacuum and mop again, obsessed with the feeling that it has been defiled.

I simply cannot allow anyone into my bedroom and I get very triggered if my children or grandchildren jump on my bed. Again, it feels like an intrusion of my personal boundaries, especially if my youngest daughter and son are messing about and I can hear her telling him to stop. They're just playing, I can hear them laughing, but it chills something deep down inside of me even though I know they're safe and only mucking about as kids should. I can't even babysit my own grandchildren overnight as I wouldn't want to take on the responsibility of looking after someone else's child. My internal self-talk is that I'm a broken, useless, terrible mother, not worthy of a good relationship or a good family, too much trouble, too complicated. I find myself apologising even when I'm not to blame so that I can avoid any kind of confrontation, even when the other person is a friend or someone I love and would never react that way.

All of this is a constant daily battle. It's exhausting. I'm shattered on the inside even if I appear 'normal' to the outside world. It's like trying to hold back a dam and I always thought it would finally break.

Throughout 2019, the compensation claim dragged on. In September of that year, my lawyer wrote to say that CICA would not be reviewing their decision as my 'symptoms had improved over some time and will continue to improve after further treatment'. My symptoms were not 'disabling'. And there is the crux for so many survivors – if we do that, if we *survive*, we are penalised. We've got better – a bit. We'll continue to get better – a bit. We're not disabled, not really. All we have, after all, is nightmares and triggers and a life full of memories of what was done to us. My solicitor suggested that I sign and accept the findings, take the compensation offered; but it was never about the money because how can you put a price on what was done to me, what is done to any victim?

All I wanted was to push and keep pushing, to have them acknowledge that this should never have been allowed to continue. Of course, Terry Price made the choice to abuse me, but there was collusion in the sense that nothing was done to stop him and the fact that he had been allowed to hide behind a name change meant that other children became victims too. Was I getting over that? No. No, I was not. The solicitor gave me another warning: if I didn't sign and accept, we'd be back to the start again. They'd look at my case from page one and I might end up with a 'less favourable decision that the original'. Honestly? I wanted to tell them all to get to Hell. I felt played and manipulated, as if I was a little girl again being told to put up or shut up.

I kept looking at the letter from CICA – it was there in black and white, but it didn't show the reality of what I was living with:

In making this award I have considered all the information provided by West Midlands Police and your medical records from [xx] Surgery. As a result, I have made an award for non-consensual penile penetration – repeated incidents over a period of up to 3 years.

There is nothing in your medical records to suggest that you will have a permanently disabling mental illness.

Non-consensual penile penetration. That didn't sound too bad, did it? And if an expert was telling me that I was fine mentally, well, who was I to question anything? I sat there, papers surrounding me, judgements from other people all deciding what had been done and what the effects had been, and I wept. My fingers flicked the little yellow Post-it stickers which pointed out from the letter, *SIGN HERE* glaring at me like a demand in an *Alice in Wonderland* book. I was drained. All I had to do was sign. All I had to do was accept that they had decided I was fine and that there was a monetary figure which would wipe the slate clean. I could sign and go on holiday, blow the money on nonsense, or save it for a rainy day.

'It's dirty money,' I whispered to myself. 'It's blood money.'

I didn't want a fancy pair of shoes that would remind me of him every time I wore them. I didn't want to lie on a beach knowing what had paid for it. I have no idea how long I sat there as the sky outside the window got darker, but the tears slowed down and the feeling of panic lessened. I didn't need a lawyer or a government body to tell me how to live and I certainly didn't need to do what they told me – I'd had enough of that. As I walked round the room, switching on one lamp after another, it was as if the light shed clarity on my decision. I wouldn't back down. If they wanted to go back to the start, I had the strength for that – I had the strength for anything.

Bring it on.

* * *

My battle with the CICA finally ended with my second and last tribunal hearing in April 2021, with new assessments, when they stated: 'The Authority acknowledged the findings contained in the medical report and addendum of Dr X as to the severity and permanence of the appellant's mental illness caused by the abuse.' While this was welcome, having to be put through yet another psychological assessment was not. I do not think that the CICA are in any way trauma informed, or in fact care that this process is retriggering and retraumatising for victims and survivors. I found it disgusting that I could get financial assistance for a walking stick if I had broken my leg, but not funding for EMDR treatment, even though it was proven that I needed it and it was not available in my area.

Life decided that I needed to have more thrown at me – this time with my mother again. It was very different to Dad's death when Mum passed. In August 2020, I was contacted out of the blue.

There had been no contact since the court case in 2017 and I had barely had any contact, apart from the one time she turned up at my house, after apparently having twins in 2007 – some short emails, letters and one Skype chat. Apart from these few instances I'd had little to no contact with her since she left for Turkey in late 2003. I was looking after Laura's kids for a few hours and the daughter of a friend of Mum's was trying to get hold of me. Laura called her for me as I just couldn't do it.

'She's passed, Mum – she's gone. She's gone.'

My initial reaction was that I wanted nothing to do with it all, but I was told that the coroner wouldn't speak to anyone else. I didn't really know her. The coroner did say it could all be passed to Social Services, but as a human being, I couldn't do that. I had to go to her house, which was awful – it was like going back to being a kid. It was stinking, cats' mess everywhere. I had to clear the house, organise the funeral, sort out all her paperwork – all the while knowing she could never now take responsibility or say sorry. The weird thing was that she had pictures everywhere of her and a little girl. She had told lots of people that she had a child in Turkey that she couldn't get back and that she was working with the Embassy to have her returned. I started to think maybe it was true, maybe I had a sister in Turkey who didn't know her mum had died, maybe everything she had told me in 2007 was true. Again, she was completely messing with my head, even in death.

Going through the paperwork she had, the files said that she had an adopted daughter in Turkey – it seemed that she had been with a man who had kids and then claimed they were twins. Her friends all thought she had actually given birth to twins. They believed her – it was crazy. No one from Turkey ever got in touch with me about Mum. I thought I would be able to cope, but it was so hard. Even with it being during the Covid-19 global pandemic, the number of people who were allowed didn't turn up, she had no one really. It turned out that it was a twisted bowel which killed her, the same problem Baby Freya had been so ill with those years ago.

Both Mum and Dad had died at the age of 64 and I would never get what I needed from either of them. Although Dad had done much better in later years, he had still failed me as a child. And Mum? Well, where would I start? She could never apologise now, but she was never the sort of woman who would have taken responsibility anyway. If she'd lived to be a hundred, she would have still acted the victim.

She never reached out to me after the trial – in fact, she didn't even tell her friends what the case was that she was giving evidence to. I've been left with a lot of unanswered questions. I have to live with the fact that I'll never get an apology but I have to hold onto the fact that at least the door is closed. For a lot of years, I made excuses for her – she'd been through the care system and hadn't experienced a good upbringing herself or had good role models. But neither did I – it's not an excuse. When you become a parent, it's up to you to break the cycle. I love my dad to pieces but he wasn't great – they were both very selfish and I've used both examples of parenting as a how-not-to guide. They've taught me how not to do it, I guess they gave me that.

My life will never be perfect. It will never all go away, but I recognise more of the bad stuff now for what it is – *not my fault*. That doesn't mean it's any easier, but I know why it's there, I know there is a direct line from what was done to me then to how I am now. My lack of personal boundaries, my inability to say 'no', means that I can't trust myself to take care of me. I can never put my own needs and wants over those of other people. I then get angry with myself for being weak and overthinking things.

I find it so hard to make healthy relationships or even make new friends – often the first thing people ask is, 'So, what do you do?' Explaining why I'm taking time out or never had a good career or finished my degree just reinforces to me that I'm not good enough. I know it would be oversharing anyway but I would feel that I needed to explain everything, explain me, and I can't do that, it's too much. I loved going to university and felt that I was finally going to turn my life around but when I had to stop halfway through, it was as if the monster was back. The monster which says I'll never amount to anything, I'll always be useless so why even bother trying? While I was at Warwick, there was such joy – but then the waves of depression came crashing down, the overwhelming sense that my mind and body just wanted to close down. I had no idea why this kept happening to me but it reinforced every negative thought about being fundamentally broken and different to everyone else.

I feel robbed by Terry Price. It is his relentless sexual and emotional abuse that gives me nightmares, flashbacks, body memories. He has even stolen beautiful experiences from me, such as the births of my children. My life would be very different if he hadn't destroyed the very core of me and that lives with me every single day: all I can do is find a way to live with it.

There are big chunks of my childhood I can't remember, they are completely blocked out. I think of it as 'trauma brain' – it's protective, but it can be infuriating. My brain jumps from being in one place to another, from being three years old to nine to six. That happens for most people in some ways, but I know that I'm blocking things rather than just remembering bits of a normal life. If you haven't suffered abuse, then you might start reflecting on when you started school, then jump to when you started high school – however, if you thought about it, you'd be able to remember the bits in between. There are huge parts of my own life I simply can't remember. There's just nothing there. It isn't a bad memory or holes in what I can remember, it is trauma brain – an actual thing which protects me from the worst of it all.

When I was giving birth to my last two kids, I was having such terrible flashbacks and I'm petrified that the same thing could happen again at any point. It was one of the most awful things I'd ever experienced as I was locked in for a long time after those births, it took ages to come out of it. People need to understand that the terrible things which were done to me are part of a list I'll always be adding to. The irony is, the stronger I get, the more memories come back to me, which take me back to square one. It's a constant cycle. I do wish I could remember it all, I wish it was all there. You think you've put some things in a box but when you open that box, or your subconscious opens it for you, you never know what is going to come out. Your whole world collapses and you're flooded with more and more. Even the police wanted it to be a nice, neat little package – extra memories which came later didn't count, they weren't included. I have night terrors of where I'm being held down, I can't breathe and Terry is saying nasty things, saying I deserve it all, but as night terrors they aren't as well formed as the ones I knew I had to remember for the case.

I shouldn't have to feel lucky that I got a conviction, I shouldn't have to feel grateful.

I have also been triggered by further abuse coverage I see in the media, particularly the Barry Bennell football abuse coverage.[2] There is a two-tier system of victims – if you've been abused by someone famous, or are indeed famous yourself, the media, the solicitors, everyone will be all over it. If you're just a normal person, you take what you're given. I know that to my cost. You're just not listened to. Campaigns wouldn't be where they are without us ordinary people.

There has to stop being this two-tier system of what matters and what the police and Crown Prosecution Service take seriously. Being sexually assaulted in my own bed wasn't enough for the police to take it seriously – but it should be. It's just another message that you're

---

2 In 2016, allegations centred on abuse of young players at two football clubs – Crewe Alexandra and Manchester City – which had been associated with Barry Bennell. Bennell had been previously convicted of sexual abuse offences in the US in 1995, and in the UK in 1998. In November 2016, he was charged with new offences. From the time the allegations were first made, hundreds of victims came forward, revealing a crisis at the heart of British football. Bennell had previously changed his name to Richard Jones, and was tried under that name. He was found guilty of 36 offences in February 2018 followed by another seven, and then finally convicted of 52. He was jailed for 31 years and expected to serve half of that, with the rest on licence. He appealed his sentence but the appeal was rejected. The Offside Trust was set up to provide support for victims of abuse in sport.

less, that you're not important enough for anyone to care. We all need to be treated equally and listened to, not just the ones who have a public profile. I still have this internal battle, feeling like there must have been something wrong with me that made me a target, but I know the reality is that it's just so prevalent. I think it was actually easier to believe it was me specifically who deserved the abuse, because that's not as scary as knowing predators are everywhere.

You're completely susceptible to being put down and minimised and for me that has been a running theme, even going back to childhood friendships. I've always been attracted to people who are louder, who will do all the talking and I won't have to; I can sort of hide. It's a protective thing, you don't want to let people too close: stay unseen, don't draw attention.

I've never really been able to talk about the abuse with partners – men just expect sex and they don't read signs when you don't want it in my experience. Sometimes I would dissociate and they wouldn't understand that or the times I cried. I've never been able to build up to a point in my head where I can say no, I don't want to – I have no boundaries out loud. There's a massive issue not spoken about if you also have that link between what was done to you as a child and enjoying sex. My first orgasm was at such a young age, not knowing what it was and my abuser telling me it was OK – I didn't realise until many years later what that was and I felt like my body had betrayed me. You feel such shame – was I actually enjoying that? It's just your body responding naturally to stimulus but it takes a while to accept that.

It takes a lifetime to accept so much, but I'm getting there.

26

DELLA'S LAW

The trial in 2017 flagged up that there was a massive issue with offenders changing their names. I hadn't heard about it before, I had no idea they could do it from prison. Terry Price changed his name by deed poll, as anyone can. It can be done online very easily and – if you are a sex offender – you are duty bound legally to inform the authorities within three days. However, as this is left down to the perpetrators, who are by their very nature manipulative and deviant, is it any wonder many change their names to hide their offending pasts, gain new identities, move towns and totally wipe their slates clean? I was told by someone from the Probation Services who came to see me after the trial that this was a huge issue. I don't think the general public has any idea – why would they? It beggars belief that prisoners can even do this. If you went up to any ordinary person on the street and told them, they would laugh in your face and yet it's happening, it's happening more than you could ever imagine.

There is no joined-up approach between the police and courts and prisons and probation. When criminals come out of prison, any restrictions are under the name that they were given in. If you're found guilty as Joe Bloggs, then it's Joe Bloggs who has restrictions placed on him. If he changes to Ian the Innocent? Well, that's all hunky dory, off you go, nothing to see here. There just aren't the resources to check them all – multi agency personnel are meant to arrive unannounced to check phones and things like that but there's not enough of them. Offenders can come out and start their new life with a new name, or they can change it when they are out in the community. They can apply for driving licences and passports in their new name, which means that when they show these as proof of identity for a Disclosure and Barring Service (DBS) check, it comes back clean. It absolutely blew my mind that during the DBS process, all they have to do is check a box to say they've never been known by any other name and that's it, no one does a follow-up! Safeguarding is a buzzword in the UK, but DBS checks aren't worth the paper they're written on.

Paedophiles are devious by nature and they know the system is broken. They know how to play that same system, to get a new bank account in their new name, a passport, driving licence, the list goes on. Prison is a school for offenders and it's absolutely apparent that this information is passed around. It's terrifying to me that these people are out there and they're abusing the system in this way.

I hear of so many cases through my work now – there was one man who abused children in the UK then, on release, changed his name. He went to Spain and became a live-in au pair and a teacher at a number of prestigious British schools. He was alleged to have abused 36 children in Spain.[3]

People know of Ian Huntley's awful crimes[4] but he should never have been able to get away with what he did in the first place. This broken system allowed it when it gave him the freedom to change his name. When Huntley applied to become a school caretaker, his background should have been scrupulously

---

3 Ben Lewis was a convicted sex offender who moved to Spain after changing his name to Ben David. He did this just two months after being given a two-year suspended sentence. He also used the name Ben Rose to apply for job vacancies. Thirty-six victims were identified in Madrid, between four and eight years of age.

4 In 2002, Ian Huntley murdered 10-year-olds Jessica Chapman and Holly Wells. During a nationwide hunt for the two girls, Huntley – a caretaker at a local college – was one of those who contributed to an appeal for their safe return. He already had a rape allegation against him and a history of sexual behaviour with young girls. Holly and Jessica were killed by him in his house – where they had gone after walking past and recognising Huntley as the partner of Maxine Carr who worked at their school.

checked but he had changed his name to Ian Nixon. Once he had the job, he changed back to Ian Huntley again. This sparked the Bichard Inquiry (2004), which identified the name change loophole, but nothing was done about it.

After Sarah Payne was murdered in July 2000[5] and Sarah's Law (the Child Sex Offender Disclosure Scheme/ CSODS) was rolled out in 2010, everyone hoped that would change things, but it's not fit for purpose. It never would be while this loophole remained. Both Sarah's Law and Clare's Law, the Domestic Violence Disclosure Scheme (DVDS), rely on the name that is put forward. So, if an offender has already changed their name when they commit more crimes to a clean one, of course it will come back as absolutely fine. Barry Bennell, Ian Huntley, Vanessa George, John Worboys ... they are all prolific sexual offenders who have changed their names. There were recommendations at the time of Huntley, and plenty of times since to look into the loophole, but it never was. There was a detailed BBC report which had an interview with a representative from the Home

---

5   Eight year old Sarah Payne was murdered by Roy Whiting. Whiting had previously abducted and sexually assaulted a nine-year-old girl. He was on the sex offenders' register when Sarah went missing and was even interviewed by police, who had insufficient evidence to charge him. Forensics tests on his car finally allowed police to charge him with the abduction and murder of Sarah. He was sentenced to life and the judge said 'life should mean life' in this case. Newspaper sources claim he plans to change his name if ever released. Sarah's mother, Sara, successfully campaigned for 'Sarah's Law', also known as the Child Sex Offender Disclosure Scheme, which allows parents, carers or guardians to formally ask the police for information about anyone who has contact with their child and who they have concerns about regarding risk.

Office, who said it was wrong in 2010.[6] How can nothing have been done since then?

After my court case, I knew I couldn't live with knowing this awful situation existed and not do anything about it. In 2018, I set up an online petition which received about 3,000 signatures, but it was such hard work to even get to that stage. I couldn't believe that was an accurate representation of how many people cared about the problem – it seemed to get no traction. There was another similar petition at the same time from a group called The Safeguarding Alliance. I approached them and said, 'We seem to be on the same page.' By this point they had been doing research for two years and the leader of the group, Emily Konstantas, had lots of results from Freedom of Information requests. Out of 43 police forces, only 16 even responded – just over a third. From those, over 900 sex offenders were missing. Emily was doing it from a statistical perspective but I could do it with a survivor's voice. We quickly found we were two sides of the same coin and were equally passionate about having the law changed.

From that point on, the media did respond to us. I did an interview with Sky,[7] which got great feedback and together we raised another petition. Unfortunately, they

6 BBC News, BBC Radio 5 live – '5 Live Investigates, Name Change Danger'.

7 https://news.sky.com/story/more-than-900-sex-offenders-disappear-from-police-radar-with-many-changing-their-names-and-not-telling-officers-12036341

didn't put up a link, nor did *The Times* or the *Mirror*. It went onto *Mumsnet* and other forums, but we lost so many opportunities for getting signatures by not having those media outlets backing us fully. It was frustrating as we'd put so much work into it, and they'd done the story well, but the lack of a link felt like a wasted opportunity. It was relentless to get the petition out, all social media was used, but for some reason it just didn't seem to get the signatures we thought it would. We got shadow banned, we had people signing who then told us that their names weren't there, a cybergroup had reported it as being a hate crime and it came up as spam on Facebook. It would be easy to fall into conspiracy theories, but I try to avoid that.

Numbers were changing – one day it was 40,000, the next, 27,000. People were trying to sign and messages were coming back saying they were using a wrong email format when they weren't. The petition ended with 37,000 signatures, much fewer than the 100,000 needed to have this debated in Parliament.

The government response at 10,000 signatures was deemed not good enough by the Petitions Committee. The government said they would only acknowledge enrolled deed polls, which is when the old name, new name and address are printed publicly rather than a simple online change where two people sign it, one as witness, and that's that. With the government saying they would move towards only accepting the former, it would make things more above board and easier to track. However, a lot of people in the trans community were very much against this. I understood their concerns but I needed to do all I could to protect children – once legislation is being drafted, other issues can be looked at, but the priority has to be the hundreds of thousands of children at risk from abuse every year.

In the next round of responses, the Police, Crime, Sentencing and Courts Bill did address this and Sarah Champion MP took it up. As did Sajid Javid, Conservative MP for Bromsgrove, alongside The Centre for Justice think tank, in their 'Safer Children' report. Rotherham child sex abuse survivor and activist Sammy Woodhouse[8] was also instrumental in highlighting this issue – I will be forever grateful to her for her input and all she does to campaign for victims and survivors.

A lot of officials and politicians say it's complicated, but surely it could just apply to convicted sex offenders? Once you cross that line, there are certain rights you should forego. It needs to stop being all about the perpetrator and start being about the victims, those blameless children who have had their innocence stolen. When will we start focusing on them and put protections in place for them rather than repeat the

---

8 Sammy Woodhouse is an activist against child sexual abuse. She helped to expose the Rotherham abuse scandal.

mistakes of the past and give the offenders power and control? Everyone thinks the Sex Offenders Register is this magic thing which protects children but it really doesn't. Every name of every sex offender in the country needs to be easily accessible to every police force in the UK, not just the offenders in their own area – these people are clever, they know how to manipulate and avoid detection, that's how they abused in the first place. Why would they stop?

Why can't it be that easy that something flags up officially when a convicted sex offender tries to change their name? The Home Office believes the police have all the answers, the police think the Home Office know it all, the Driver and Vehicle Licensing Authority (DVLA) believe that name changes are nothing to do with them, the Passport Office doesn't ask for the enrolled registration and the Disclosure and Barring Service (DBS) simply have a ticking box exercise on our children's safety. A passport is an official document that allows offenders to travel anywhere to abuse, and they do!

Rape is virtually decriminalised and rapists, abusers, can act with impunity – and the fact that they can change their name makes it even easier. I want Della's Law to bring sex offenders to account – it wouldn't affect anyone else's freedoms. The question would be simple: are you a sex offender? Yes? Then this applies to you. Are you not a sex offender? No? Then this isn't applicable and your rights won't be affected at all, other than safeguarding being made stronger.

Recently, BBC drama series *Holby City*'s writers highlighted the journey victims and survivors go through, well into adulthood. The scriptwriters wrote the name change loophole into the storyline involving a predator who was procuring young girls for wealthy clients. They did an amazing job in getting this storyline out into the wider public, I appreciated it hugely. With the interest of Sky News as well as all of the newspaper coverage, and now being taken up by MPs, the campaign feels so much bigger than me. It's huge and it can sometimes feel quite overwhelming.

When, in June 2021, the Government agreed to have a parliamentary debate on Della's Law, I was delighted – finally, something was happening, finally the loophole would be uncovered by those in power. The Government said they would come back in a year with the name change review findings. The Safeguarding Alliance was included in this review panel, not only to ensure transparency, but also because they know this loophole inside out. They have commissioned a very comprehensive report themselves and will ensure my voice as their ambassador is heard and my story used as a force to drive change.

In March 2022, MP Sarah Champion asked that the government review findings be put in the public domain, only to be told that the review was nearly completed, but wouldn't be made public. Sarah said she'd follow this up and try to change this. Since then, I've been contacted by so many survivors who have told me that they're in similar positions. One woman was abused by her father and, after he served half his sentence, immediately changed his name on release. These stories were breaking my heart, but at least I knew that the review was ongoing.

But in August 2022, the government admitted the review had been concluded and it would not be made public. Their reason was that it was an internal review, which meant it didn't need to be released – something they hadn't said at the start. I was so optimistic when the plan was to look at all of the departments – the DVLA, the Passport Office and more – to develop joined-up legislation on this. It felt massive and yet, now, I'd had the door slammed in my face again. I was shattered.

Where do I go from here? I'm back to contacting all MPs, I'm back to telling everyone about Della's Law – I'm back to square one, really. I've come so far, and now what? The government needs to be transparent and look at how these name changes affect policy moving forward, and they need to do it soon, because every delay puts another child at risk. Am I dejected, am I disappointed? Of course – but I've dug deep into my own strength before and I'll do it again. I can't just walk away and it's a battle I'll fight until I win.

I've almost become numb in telling my story and giving journalists the bare bones for their story of mine. The driving force is an enormous responsibility, but also I have a personal responsibility as I know about this – no one else up until now has campaigned with my background and experiences. I'll keep on until the law is changed. I do think people are listening now but I can't get complacent. I can't take my foot off the pedal. It can't get lost, I have to keep chipping away. I could get lost in the size of it, but when I think of how many children have already been affected, and are undoubtedly being affected right now, then I know I have to keep going.

I don't see it as my name, I associate Della's Law with the little six-year-old girl whose picture they use to illustrate the story. I do it for her. She symbolises everything for me, I wish I could go back and tell her that she's going to get through. There's little me and big me – we're attached and I find that hard.

*** *

It could become overwhelming. I do just want some peace and a rest. Maybe I'll get some for me one day – a campervan and off to do Route 66! That would be the dream, getting me back again; no, getting me for the first time, really.

I need to think that I can start over now – I can create myself, learn new things, new experiences. My experiences shone a light onto something I wasn't aware of and this is now a cause I need to see my way through, that's all I can take from this. I used to think I was on my own and I was walking a lonely road; I felt that for a long time. We all have a voice and by us speaking, we give that power to the next person to know they have a voice too. The more people talk about it, the more normal it becomes. While we don't talk about child abuse, it stays a dirty secret. People shut you down because it's so hard for them to hear. I've tried throughout my life so many times and the more it's shut down, the more it becomes internalised and you think it's your fault. Only through talking can we learn, change policies and put safeguarding in place. I can either close down or I can run with this. I don't want a solid rock of hate inside me, I want to open up and in doing so, find there are other people who find their voices by hearing me.

I hope that social workers, teachers, school nurses, GPs, youth workers and police officers will read this book. I want to say to them, *you are on the front line and your empathy, understanding, early intervention and action could be what the child in front of you needs to break the cycle of abuse for them.* I hope government officials and policymakers read this book. I want to say to them, *you have the power and the wherewithal to make real and effective change. Research already shows that pounds spent in early intervention in childhood saves huge amounts later in life. We know so much already, but failure to put services in place is truly a false economy.*

I hope academics and university professors read this book. I want to say to them, *you are the ones who can push for research into the links between early trauma and the adverse life-long, life-limiting physical and mental health outcomes for victims and survivors who have been subjected to all forms of abuse in childhood; I'm begging you to do it.*

It truly does take a village to raise a child, it is the responsibility of all of us to ensure that village is a safe, nurturing and inclusive environment for every little one out there. If it isn't? Well, then, we, collectively and individually, must play our part in changing that or accept that we have colluded in abuse.

Time and time again, I hear people saying, '*someone* should do something about that'. I want to remind you, *we* are that someone, you, me, *us*. We can climb mountains when the cause is important enough, but we need to prepare for battle because children are relying on us.

I'm relying on *you*.

* * *

I was trapped for so long. Trapped with a mother who didn't care, who put me in danger and turned a blind eye to the horrific abuse I endured. I was trapped in a life which had given me those foundations, which had told me I was nothing and I deserved only bad things. I was trapped in a system which washed its hands of me as a child and as a woman carrying the burden of her past. I was trapped in relationships which made me feel worthless and which perpetuated the cycle of abuse. I was trapped in my shame and in my worthlessness.

Now I'm no longer trapped. I am a woman who knows her power and I know that I can do great things. I won't be silenced any longer. I'll scream and shout and I'll make this world a better place for the little ones who come after me. What I endured can never be changed, but what I achieve is all down to me.

There's an army of us. The broken, the beaten, the used and exploited. The fact that we're still standing shows our strength, but the fact that we want to keep fighting, to take on even more demons, to fight even more wars, is a miracle.

I'm not the sum of what was done to me.

I am a warrior and every fibre of my being will fight until there isn't a breath in my body.

Come with me – we can do this.

EPILOGUE

I didn't ask to be abused.

I didn't deserve to be abused.

I didn't want to be abused.

All of that was out of my control, but I control the life I have now. It's not easy and it's not constant, but it's what I have.

I tell myself, *look in the mirror and be proud. You're still here and that's more than you sometimes thought was ever possible.*

There were so many times when I didn't want to get up.

But I did.

There were days when I thought I just couldn't go on.

But I did.

There were memories which I thought I could never endure.

But I did.

I survived it all and I'll survive whatever there is to come. I'm not saying there won't be dark times, that there won't be nights that seem never-ending, challenges like mountains, battles which knock the breath from me – but I'll conquer them. I have to. It's who I am.

I'll push on.

I'll fight another day.

And there will come a time when I look back and will finally be able to say to little Della, *we did it, we made a difference.*

ACKNOWLEDGEMENTS

I always knew I had to write a book, but without the help, support and guidance from the following people, I fear it might never have come to fruition. Thank you all, you have touched my heart in ways I cannot explain, you have given me a voice that I thought I would never be brave enough to use and you have shown me that together, we can do anything.

To my family, thank you for keeping me here. There have been many times that I didn't think I could take another day, but knowing I have you, knowing what a hole I would leave in your lives if I did end it, has kept me grounded and wanting to fight. Laura, James, Charlie and Ellie, my four children, you have taught me so much about life, what being a parent is and should be, and given me my best days in watching you grow. Ian and Naomi, thank you for loving my children and being the best parents to my grandchildren. My grandchildren Freya, Archie, Jacob and Freddie (and those yet to be), I love watching the world through your beautiful innocent eyes, full of wonder and excitement. Every day, you show me what life looks like when you have a loving and nurturing home that allows you to flourish and become anything you want to be.

When I lost Dad, I found my family in Aunty Bernie and Aunty Donna, two amazingly strong and beautiful women – you've faced your own battles, but still remained steadfast and soft. Life could have hardened you, but you were and are better than that, true inspirational women for us all to look up to. My love for you and your families is immense. I have to thank your daughters Claire, Carrie-ann and Kirsty for supporting the campaign for #DellasLaw too. The hours you put in online and walking the streets handing out flyers and educating the public truly touched my heart. Your care for our children and their safety is a powerhouse; together, we will do this. To Uncle John, thank you for the phone calls, picking up the baton where Dad left. You sound just like him too, which was hard at first, but I know how blessed I am to have you.

Dear Katie, you have been a constant stream of

positivity and love, for that I thank you. Claire, wow what a journey! We met through music all those years ago and here you are, forever in my corner, sending the most inspirational and comforting gifts and just being the wackiest, truest friend a girl could want. Carole (Toots) – you, my love, are one of the most generous, beautiful souls I have been fortunate to meet on my journey, a true earth mother with a heart as big as the sun. Tracy, my childhood friend, I have always loved that we can go years without seeing each other and just pick up where we left off – every girl needs a friend like you, that's why you will always be surrounded by many. Em Zii, for someone I've never met in 'real life', you have been amazing. Once you heard about the campaign for #DellasLaw, you went over and above to get the petition out there. Even spending hours writing to influencers, media and anyone that would listen, because you cared so deeply about safeguarding children. I will be forever grateful to you. Kerry, an activist and all-round amazing human being, thank you for showing me what 37,000 people looked like, just when I thought I had failed with the petition.

To my fellow campaigners, whom I think of as my survivor family, I thank you for giving me a voice, for showing that by internalising our hurt we further silence our little selves, and that by speaking out, we hold out a beacon for others to take up and run with.

Danny Wolstencroft (Lads_Like_Us) – anyone who hears you speak will be forever changed. Your raw honesty is like a comforting blanket that allows others to speak their truths and know they are no longer alone, thank you.

Chris Tuck (Survivors of Abuse) – you have made it your life's work to ensure that child sexual abuse and child abuse in all its forms is spoken about, you work tirelessly to evoke change from within government and you selflessly travel the country to support others in their campaigns too, all while running your own charity supporting victims and survivors and promoting health and wellness. Thank you.

Phillip Lafferty (Voicing CSA) – you have given so many of us a safe space to speak, feel supported and make lifelong friendships. Your meetings bridged the gap between professionals and victims/survivors, the likes of which I have never experienced before, enabling us to educate the educators. Such a beautiful, driven and honourable man, thank you.

Shell (A Ritual Abuse Survivor's Poetry) – your tenacity, your poetry and your education around DID (dissociative identity disorder) and SRA (Satanic ritual abuse) is incredible, thank you.

Pauline (Take Cover) – I will always be so grateful for your friendship and beautiful photography, showing life after abuse can be beautiful.

Caryn Walker (author of her own book, *Tell Me You're Sorry, Daddy*) – it was meeting you that spurred me on to write this book. You taught me so much about courage in adversity and doing it anyway, thank you.

David Lean – your fight for justice opened the floodgates for other victims and survivors of abuse in football to come forward. I will be forever grateful that because of your bravery, my grandchildren will be safer to enjoy the beautiful game.

Mandy and Mickey (Nottingham CSA Survivors support) – sadly, Mickey is no longer with us, but his fight goes on through his survivor family in Nottingham. Mandy, thank you for everything you do and have done to get justice and change.

Mike (Lads_Like_Us) – you have always been there at the end of any message, to offer hope and support with my campaign. Your quest along with Danny, to educate the educators and help other men to see there is hope and life after abuse is incredible, thank you.

To RoSA and RSVP, two charities that are very dear to me. Without you at key moments in my journey, I'm not sure I could have carried on. Your work is invaluable and your drive to be as inclusive as possible and support those in hard-to-reach places is testament to your drive to give us a better chance at life during and after abuse.

Emily Konstantas and your amazing team at The Safeguarding Alliance – until our paths crossed I felt like a tiny drop in the ocean, trying to get my campaign to stop sex offenders changing their names out into the wider public arena. Together, we have broken down many barriers to getting this law changed. We have amassed so much media coverage, no one in government can say they did not know and we have finally got those in power to sit up and take notice. We are two sides of the same coin, we are a united powerhouse and we simply will not stop until this law is changed. I know we can and will do this, failure is simply not an option! Thank you for standing by my side, as I stand by yours.

To the families of Holly Wells and Jessica Chapman, I'm so sorry you were failed. Huntley should never have been able to get that job and your beautiful girls should have been protected and kept safe to grow and flourish. To the families of Sarah Payne and Clare Wood, you are constantly on my mind as I push for Della's Law. I understand through my own fight how hard you fought to get Sarah's Law and Clare's Law into being – I only hope that Della's Law can strengthen them both and that they are finally fit for purpose, in that perpetrators cannot hide behind name changes to avoid detection.

My thoughts are turned to all those brave victims

and survivors who couldn't stay, who were so consumed and overwhelmed by the burden of having to carry the weight of child sexual abuse that they had to leave to find some peace. I thank you for doing your absolute best to stay in a world that seems to favour perpetrators.

To all those who've been supportive and vocal about #DellasLaw – Sarah Champion MP, Sajid Javid MP, Maria Rubia (Fragma), Olivia Robey (CSJ Think Tank) and Dr Jessica Taylor, thank you. Many shy away from the subject, but you have all gone over and above to raise public awareness and in doing so, pushed for this law to be changed. A special mention to Sammy Woodhouse: thank you for running with this and putting it in front of those who have the power to change it. I will always remember our chat when I said, *'Sometimes this just feels too big, like the more you know, the more you realise how massive a problem it is.'* And you said, *'Della, if we didn't keep on chipping away, how would anything change?'* That sticks with me and continues to drive me on, on days when I feel like giving up. Thank you.

I'd also like to thank those who will never realise the impression they made on my life and the lives of thousands of others. Dr Bessel van der Kolk, Gabor Maté and Maya Angelou, you have taught me so much about life as a victim and survivor of abuse, about trauma, about self-help, about acknowledging little Della and all she has suffered and overcome. About seeing myself as a brave and powerful warrior, rather than simply broken.

Lastly, and most importantly to me, with regards to you reading this right now is my deep gratitude to Linda Watson-Brown. Linda, without your patience, determination, prompting and understanding of me and my life story, this book simply would not have been written. You've not only 'gotten' me completely, you've also educated me along the way and brought many more incredible authors, activists and change makers onto my radar. Thank you so much for everything, you beautiful soul, you.

Beth Eynon and all at John Blake Publishing – thank you for believing in me, my story and the campaign. It's because people like you give people like me a chance that change is possible, thank you.

The Survivors Trust has a very useful webpage where you can find specialist support in your local area by putting in your postcode: www.thesurvivorstrust.org.

To the 37,000 people who signed the petition, I will never be able to thank you personally, but know that I appreciate every single one of you. If you visit www.thesafeguardingalliance.org.uk, you will be able to keep up to date with the campaign and also sign up to support Della's Law.

From the bottom of my heart, thank you to everyone above and to everyone reading my story – you've given me a voice and you've given that lost little girl a voice. We'll never be trapped again x